THE ETERNAL GALILEAN

The Eternal Galilean

FULTON J. SHEEN, PhD, DD, LlD

*Agrégé en Philosophie de L'Université de Louvain and
The Catholic University of America*

ALBA·HOUSE NEW·YORK

SOCIETY OF ST. PAUL, 2187 VICTORY BLVD., STATEN ISLAND, NEW YORK 10314

ST PAULS

Library of Congress Cataloging-in-Publication Data

Sheen, Fulton J. (Fulton John), 1895-1979.
    The eternal Galilean / Fulton J. Sheen.
        p.   cm.
    "Revised to incorporate a more recent and more recognizable
  translation of the Scripture text" — T.p. verso.
    ISBN 0-8189-0774-6
    1. Jesus Christ — Biography — Devotional literature. 2. Jesus
  Christ — Person and offices — Devotional literature. 3. Catholic
  Church — Doctrines.   I. Title.
  BT306.5.S48   1997
  232.9'01 — dc21   96-54829
  [B]   CIP

Nihil Obstat:
  Arthur J. Scanlan, STD
  Censor Librorum
Imprimatur:
  ✠ Patrick Cardinal Hayes
  Archbishop of New York
  March 11, 1934

The Nihil Obstat and Imprimatur are official declarations that a book or
pamphlet is free of doctrinal or moral error. No implication is contained
therein that those who have granted the Nihil Obstat and Imprimatur
agree with the contents, opinions or statements expressed.

ISBN: 0-8189-0774-6

Originally published in March, 1934 with © copyright 1934 by D.
Appleton-Century Company, Inc. This edition had seven printings before
the issuance of a Popular Library Edition, Garden City, New York in
October of 1954. This edition went through at least four printings.
Editions were also published in Italy, Poland, Ireland and Great Britain.

This Alba House edition is produced by special arrangement
with the Estate of Fulton J. Sheen and the Society for the
Propagation of the Faith, 366 Fifth Avenue, New York, NY 10001. It has
been revised to incorporate a more recent and more recognizable
translation of the Scripture texts.

This book is published in the United States of America
by Alba House, the publishing arm of the Society of St. Paul,
an international religious congregation of priests and brothers
serving the Church through the communications media.

Printing Information:

Current Printing - first digit   1 2 3 4 5 6 7 8 9 10

Year of Current Printing - first year shown

1997 1998 1999 2000 2001 2002 2003 2004 2005

Contents

Biblical Abbreviations

OLD TESTAMENT

Genesis	Gn	Nehemiah	Ne	Baruch	Ba
Exodus	Ex	Tobit	Tb	Ezekiel	Ezk
Leviticus	Lv	Judith	Jdt	Daniel	Dn
Numbers	Nb	Esther	Est	Hosea	Ho
Deuteronomy	Dt	1 Maccabees	1 M	Joel	Jl
Joshua	Jos	2 Maccabees	2 M	Amos	Am
Judges	Jg	Job	Jb	Obadiah	Ob
Ruth	Rt	Psalms	Ps	Jonah	Jon
1 Samuel	1 S	Proverbs	Pr	Micah	Mi
2 Samuel	2 S	Ecclesiastes	Ec	Nahum	Na
1 Kings	1 K	Song of Songs	Sg	Habakkuk	Hab
2 Kings	2 K	Wisdom	Ws	Zephaniah	Zp
1 Chronicles	1 Ch	Sirach	Si	Haggai	Hg
2 Chronicles	2 Ch	Isaiah	Is	Malachi	Ml
Ezra	Ezr	Jeremiah	Jr	Zechariah	Zc
		Lamentations	Lm		

NEW TESTAMENT

Matthew	Mt	Ephesians	Eph	Hebrews	Heb
Mark	Mk	Philippians	Ph	James	Jm
Luke	Lk	Colossians	Col	1 Peter	1 P
John	Jn	1 Thessalonians	1 Th	2 Peter	2 P
Acts	Ac	2 Thessalonians	2 Th	1 John	1 Jn
Romans	Rm	1 Timothy	1 Tm	2 John	2 Jn
1 Corinthians	1 Cor	2 Timothy	2 Tm	3 John	3 Jn
2 Corinthians	2 Cor	Titus	Tt	Jude	Jude
Galatians	Gal	Philemon	Phm	Revelation	Rv

THE INFINITY OF LITTLENESS

I

THE INFINITY OF LITTLENESS

HOW CAN SOULS find GOD? It is a psychological fact that it is only by being little that we ever discover anything big. This law raised to the spiritual level tells us how we can find the immense God, and that is by having the spirit of little children. Verify this law by an appeal to personal experience and then see how it applies to God.

In the physical order have you ever noticed that to a child everything seems big: his father is bigger than any other man in the world, and his uncle who is standing near the window is taller than the great oaks down in the valley. Every child loves the story of Jack and the bean stalk, because for him every bean stalk towers up to the very skies. Now, as a matter of fact, bean stalks do not scrape the stars, but to a child they do, because the child is so small that in relation to himself everything is big — even the bean stalk. It is only when the child grows big that bean stalks become small. *It is only by being little that we ever discover anything big.*

Take another example. Every child loves to

play horse with a broomstick. He straddles it and by some peculiar magic its one wooden leg changes into four beating hoofs, and its straws into a mane whistling in every wind. Now broomsticks are not horses, and their straw is not a mane; but to a child they are, because he is so small that in comparison to himself everything else seems big. Even his giants that trample down forests like grass are creations of humility. It is only when he grows to be a big, big man that the giants die and his fairy tales become nonsense. *It is only by being little that we ever discover anything big.*

Take a final example. In many a home, a boy is playing with little tin soldiers no more than three inches high. He lines them up under the commands of lieutenants, majors, and generals and sends them out to fight the foe. To him these soldiers are not tin, they are flesh and blood; they are not three inches high but six feet tall; they are not carrying toy guns, they are firing machine guns; they are not standing still, they are going "over the top." He can smell the smoke of battle, hear the bursting shells, feel the breaking shrapnel and see men falling in death beside him. The very red of the carpet is the blood of the battlefield, as the long-range guns turn the poppy fields into Haceldamas[1] of blood! *It is a real*

---

[1] From the Aramaic meaning "field of blood," referring to the potter's field which was purchased with the blood money that Judas acquired for turning Jesus over to His enemies.

war, and there will be no peace until it's over! When he gets bigger he will stop playing, and the soldiers will only be broken tin toys, as they shrink from six feet to three inches and are gathered into a waste basket and carted away with the boyhood joys which never come back again.

What does it mean to be a child? "To be a child is to be something far different from the man of today. It is to have a spirit yet streaming from the waters of baptism; it is to believe in love, to believe in loveliness, to believe in belief; it is to be so little that the elves can reach to whisper in your ears; it is to turn pumpkins into coaches, and mice into horses; lowness into loftiness and nothingness into everything, for each child has its fairy godmother in its own soul; it is to live in a nutshell and count yourself the king of infinite space. The universe is his box of toys. He dabbles his fingers in the day-fall. He is gold-dusty by tumbling amidst the stars. He makes brief mischief with the moon. The meteors muzzle their noses in his hands. He teases the growling and kennelled thunder, and laughs at the shaking of its fiery chain. He dances in and out of the gate of heaven. His floor is littered with broken fancies. He runs wild over the fields of ether. He chases the rolling world. He gets between the feet of the horses of the sun. He stands in the lap of Mother Nature, and twines her loosened tresses after a hundred willful fashions to see in which way she will look most beautiful."[2] That is what it means to be a child. That, too, is why it is only by being little that we ever discover anything big.

Now there is a close relation between physical littleness, which is childhood, and mental littleness, which is humility. We cannot always be children, but we can always have the vision of children, which is another way of saying we can be humble. And so in the spiritual order the law remains ever the same: if a man is ever to discover anything big, he must always be making himself little; if he magnifies his ego to the infinite, he will discover nothing, for there is nothing bigger than the infinite; but, if he reduces his ego to zero, then he will discover everything big — for there is nothing smaller than himself. How then shall man discover God at Christmas time? How shall he find the reason for the joy behind the joy? Just as it is only by being little that he discovers anything big, so it is only by being humble that he will find an Infinite God in the form of a little Child.

To grasp this truth, imagine two men entering the cave where the Babe is born — one a proud man, the other a humble man. First, let the proud man, intoxicated with pride, and full of a smattering of knowledge gleaned from some handy Wellsian history of the world, enter the cave of Bethlehem. Do you think he would ever discover the immense God?

---

[2] Francis Thompson, *Essay on Shelley*.

Why, he is so big that he thinks there is nothing bigger than himself, and so wise that there is nothing wiser than himself, and so self-sufficient that nothing could ever add to his sufficiency. He is so big mentally, that to him everything else is little. To him what is really bigger than the universe is only a babe wrapped in swaddling clothes, and what is really a King is no bigger than the head of an ox, and what is really eternal Wisdom is only a speechless organism. He smiles at the credulity of the shepherds who believe in angels, and at the ignorance of the Wise Men who believe in the Providential guiding of a star. He lifts his eyebrows at the Virgin Mother, vaguely remembering an Egyptian legend about Krishna. He condescends a glance at Joseph, the man of rags, to whom the innkeeper rightly denied entrance. He thinks of all that science has done to master the earth, and then how foolish it is to think of that Babe as a Creator; he dwells on Relativity, and then on the absurdity of calling a glorified amoeba the Lord of Heaven and earth; he recalls how much Birth Control has done to keep the poor from bringing children into the world, and then how foolish was the Mother of that Child who could offer Him only a stable and a few straws from a threshing floor. He missed the infinite because he was proud; he missed discovering God because he was too big. For it is only by being little that we ever discover anything big even God.

Now let a humble man enter that cave — a man who believes he does not know everything, a man who is teachable, a man who is simple. He looks at exactly the same spectacle the proud man looked at, and yet he sees something different. He looks at the roof of the stable and sees the great canopy of stars; he looks at a Babe, and sees the One whom not even the heavens or earth could contain; he looks at a manger, and sees that God became Man to be our food. To him, those baby eyes see through hearts and read secrets unto judgment; to him, the swaddling bands which now bind life are those which later on will be broken, for life cannot be held by death; to him, the ruddy lips are those whose kiss gives immortality and whose articulation carries the message of peace and pardon. To him, the tiny hands are those on which are poised all the nations of the earth as the least grain in the balance. The date is December twenty-fifth, but to this humble man, it is Christmas; the manger is a throne; the straw is royal plumage; the stable is a castle; and the Babe is God. He found Wisdom because he was foolish, Power because he was weakness, and the Infinite, Immense and Eternal God, because he was little — *for it is only by being little that we ever discover anything big.*

Only the humble man, from another point of view, realizes he stands in need of help from above. Hence only the humble man understands the meaning of the Incarnation. It will be recalled that the word "incarnation," derived from the Latin, means "in the flesh." Sometimes, when we wish to emphasize the virtue of an individual, e.g., kindness, we say in an exaggerated manner, that that person is kindness incarnate. By that we mean that the Ideal of Kindness has taken on a human form in him or her. Now when we speak of the Incarnation we really mean that the Life, the Truth and the Love of the Perfect God took on a visible human likeness in the Person of Our Lord and Savior, Jesus Christ.

The faith of the humble man tells him: this Child is the Incarnate Word, true God and true man; He is the Creator of the human race become man; He needs milk to nourish Him, but it is by His hand that the birds of the heavens are fed; He is born of a Mother, but He is the One who preexisted His own Mother and therefore He made her beautiful and sinless, as we would have done for our own mother if we but had the power; He lies upon straw on earth and yet sustains the universe and reigns in Heaven; He is born in time, and yet He existed before all time; Maker of the stars under the stars; Ruler of the earth an outcast of earth; filling the world, lying in a manger. And yet the proud man sees only a Babe. But the humble man, illumined by faith, sees two lives in this Babe in the unity of the Person of God. Between these two lives of Christ — the Divine which He ever possesses by His eternal birth in the bosom of the Father; and the human which He began to possess by His Incarnation in the bosom of a Virgin — there is neither mingling nor confusion. The Divine in Him does not absorb the human; the human does not lessen the Divine. The union is such that there is but a single Person, the Divine Person, which is the Person of the Word of God. There is no human analogy for it — not even the union of our body and our soul in the unity of our person tells us the depths of the mystery of a God who became a Man, in order that man might become once more the image of and likeness of God.

The humble, simple souls, who are little enough to see the bigness of God in the littleness of a Babe, are therefore the only ones who will ever understand the reason of His visitation. He came to this poor earth of ours to carry on an exchange; to say to us, as only the Good God could say: "You give me your humanity, and I will give you my Divinity; you give me your time, and I will give you my eternity; you give me your weary body, and I will give you Redemption; you give me your broken heart, and I will give you Love; you give me your nothingness, and I will give you My All."

The world, which is so bent on power, never seems thoroughly to grasp the paradox that as only little children discover the bigness of the universe, so only the humble of heart ever find the greatness of God. The World misses the lesson because it confuses littleness with weakness, childlikeness with childishness, and humility with an inferiority complex. It thinks of power only in terms of physical force, and of wisdom only in terms of the vain knowledge of the spirit of the day. It forgets that great moral strength may be hidden in physical weakness, as Omnipotence was wrapped in swaddling bands; and that great Wisdom may be found in simple faith as the Eternal Mind was found in the form of a Babe. There is strength — strength before which the angels trembled, strength before which the stars prostrated, and strength before which the very throne of Herod shook in fear. It was the strength of that Divine and Awful Love which shrank from nothing to convince us of God's measure of what is really great and high.

But His law must be our law. We must begin our eternal work as He was pleased to begin His, namely, by beginning at the lowest and the humblest as the starting point for the highest and the mightiest. As He who is God descended even to the lowliness of childhood, as the first step to His everlasting triumph, so must we descend from our ignorant pride to the level of what we are in His eyes. "Unless you... become as little children," is His characteristic word, "you shall not enter into the kingdom of heaven" (Mt 18:3). To become as little children means nothing more than humility or truthfulness in judgment about ourselves, a recognition of the disproportion between our poor life and the eternal life before us, an acknowledgment of our weakness, our frailty, our sin, the poorness of all we are doing now, and yet the power and wisdom which is to be ours, provided we are humble enough to kneel before a Babe in a manger of straw, and confess Him to be Our Lord, Our Life and Our All.

Thus the birthday of the God-Man is the children's day, in which age, like a crab, turns backwards, in which the wrinkles are smoothed by the touch of a recreating hand, in which the proud become children, and the big become little, and all find their God. Hence I speak not in words of learned wisdom, but in the words of a child. We all go stooping into the cave; we put off our worldly wisdom, our pride, our seeming superiority and we become as little ones before the incalculable mystery of the humiliation of the Son of God. As such, we creep to the knee of the loveliest woman in all the world, the woman who alone of all women wears the red rose of motherhood and the white rose of virginity, the mother who in begetting Our Lord became the Mother of Men; and we ask her to teach us how to serve God, how to love God, how to pray to God. We say to her:

> Lovely Lady dressed in blue —
> Teach me how to pray.
> God was just your little Boy;

Tell me what to say!
Did you lift Him up sometimes
Gently on your knee?
Did you sing to Him the way
Mother does to me?
Did you hold His hand at night?
Did you ever try
Telling Him stories of the world?
O — And did He cry?
Do you really think He cares
If I tell Him things —
Little things that happen? And
Do the angels' wings make a noise?
Can He hear me if I speak low —
Does He understand me now?
Tell me, for you know.
Lovely Lady dressed in blue,
Teach me how to pray!
God was just your little Boy,
And you know the way.[3]

Then, when we have asked Mary how to pray,
we go to Jesus, and if we have not lost anything of
that littleness by which we discover the secrets of the
Infinite, we will ask Him one of the most important
questions in all the world. We will not ask Him how
the atoms behave, nor if space is curved, nor if light
is a wave, but we will ask Him how it feels for the

---

[3] From *The Child on His Knees*, by Mary Dixon Thayer. By
permission of The Macmillan Company, publishers.

God of Heaven to live as a Child on this poor earth
of ours.

> Little Jesus, wast Thou shy
> Once, and just so small as I?
> And what did it feel like to be
> Out of Heaven, and just like me?
> I should think that I would cry
> For my house all made of sky;
> And at waking 'twould distress me
> Not an angel there to dress me!
> Hadst Thou ever any toys,
> Like us little girls and boys?
> And didst Thou play in Heaven with all
> The angels that were not too tall,
> With stars for marbles? Did the things
> Play "Can you see me?" through their wings?
> And did Thy Mother let Thee spoil
> Thy robes, with playing on our soil?
> How nice to have them always new
> In Heaven, because 'twas quite clean blue!
> And did Thy Mother at the night
> Kiss Thee, and fold the clothes in right?
> And didst Thou feel quite good in bed,
> Kissed and sweet, and Thy prayers said?
> Thou canst not have forgotten all
> That it feels like to be small:
> So …
> Take me by the hand and walk,
> And listen to my baby talk.
> To Thy Father show my prayer
> (He will look, Thou art so fair)

And say: "O Father, I, Thy Son,
Bring the prayer of a little one."
And He will smile, that children's tongue
Has not changed since Thou wast young![4]

If we are little enough to do these things about
a crib where there clashed and thundered "unthink-
able wings around an incredible star," then we shall
discover the Infinite; if we are humble enough to go
to One who has no home, then we shall find our
home; if we are simple enough to become children
by being reborn in our old age, then we shall
discover the Life that abides when time shall be no
more. To some He comes when their hearts are
empty of the world; to others He comes when their
hungry bodies testify to the hunger of their spirits;
to others He comes when joy possesses them as truly
as an embrace; to others He comes when the world
on which they leaned as a staff has pierced their
hands; to others He comes only when tears stream
their cheeks, that He might wipe them away. But to
each and every one He comes in His own sweet way:
He — Christ; at Christ's Mass; on Christmas morn.

---

[4] Francis Thompson, *Ex Ore Infantium*.

SHEPHERDS AND WISE MEN

II

SHEPHERDS AND WISE MEN

ANY MIND WHICH THINKS about religion at all asks itself such questions as these: Why do so few souls ever find Christ? Why do the passing fads of the day win so many adherents, and the Divine Savior so few? Many there are who know Christ as a genial preacher of good fellowship, or as a social reformer of humanitarian leanings, but few there are who ever find Him as God among men, the Light and the Life of the world.

Why should such an attitude exist toward One who came to remake a world by remaking a human heart? The reason is that the minds who seek Him are either not simple enough or they are not learned enough. From the beginning Our Blessed Lord has been found only by two classes: those who know, and those who do not know — but never by those who think that they know. Divinity is so profound that it can be grasped only by the extremes of simplicity and wisdom. There is something in common between the wise and the simple, and that is humility. The wise man is humble because he knows that regardless of how deep he digs, Divinity is always deeper; the simple man is humble, because he knows Divinity is so deep there is no use digging. But that self-wise inquirer, with a sophomoric mind stuffed with the pride of his little learning, is so convinced of his knowledge that he will not dig because he thinks nothing can be deeper than himself.

As it was in the beginning, so it is now and ever shall be: Our Lord is discovered only by the simple and the learned, but never by the man with one book, never by the mind that thinks that it knows. Go back to that night when Divine Light, in order to illumine the darkness of men, tabernacled Himself in the world He had made, and you will see that only the simple and the learned found Him, namely, the shepherds and the Wise Men. The angels and a star caught up the reflection of that Light, as a torch lighted by a torch, and passed it on to the watchers of sheep and the searchers of skies. And lo! as the shepherds watched their flocks about the hills of Bethlehem, they were shaken by the light of the angels saying to them: "Fear not, for behold, I bring you good news which will give great joy to the whole nation, because this day a Savior, who is the Messiah, the Lord, has been born for you in the city of David" (Lk 2:10-11). And lo! as Wise Men from beyond the land of Media and Persia searched the heavens, the brilliance of a star, like a tabernacle lamp in the sanctuary of God's creation, beckoned them on to the stable where the star seemed to lose its light in the unearthly brilliance of the Light of the World. Like moths to the flame came the shepherds and Wise Men to a throne that was only a stable and a God that was only a Babe. And as God in the form of a Babe looked up from His crib, He saw the types of the only two classes of people who found Him that night, and who will find Him unto the end: the shepherds and the Wise Men — the simple and the learned.

The shepherds were the simple souls who knew nothing of the politics of the world, nothing of its art, nothing of its literature. Not one of them could recite a single line of Virgil, though there was hardly an educated person in the Roman Empire who was ignorant of his poetry. Into their fields and simple lives, there never came a rumor of the scandals of Herod's voluptuous court, nor even a word about the learned Gamaliel, who sat in the Temple counting out the seventy weeks of years. The great broad world of public opinion ignored them as of no account in the progress of men and nations. And yet these simple shepherds, whose early kings were shepherds, *did know* two very important things: the God above their heads, and the sheep about their feet. But that was enough for simple souls to know, and on that night when the heavens were so bright that they burst to reveal their radiant minstrelsies, an angel announced that He for whom they yearned with breathless expectancy was now born among common people in a common stable, in the common little town of Bethlehem. And gathering one of the things they knew, a little lamb, they brought it and laid it at the feet of the only other thing they knew — the God of the Heavens who came to earth as the Lamb slain from the beginning of the world. At last the shepherds had found their Shepherd.

The other class who found Him were Wise Men — not kings but teachers of kings, no mere dilettantes in knowledge, but searchers of the heavens and discoverers of the stars. In both science and religion they held first rank in their nations, the kings consulting them before they went to war, and the peasants before they tilled their land. One night a new star appeared in the heavens. Thousands of others besides the Wise Men saw its brilliant light, but these thousands were not wise with the wisdom of the Wise Men; they were wise only in their conceit. They saw only a star, but these first scientists of the Christian age saw a star and envisaged a God. To the proud man the star is only a star; but to the wise man the star is a handiwork of God — a telltale and a revelation of something beyond. And so they followed the light of the star, but instead of leading them over the mountains beyond the sun and the shining chandeliers of the Pleiades to the hid battlements of heaven, it rather led them along the sandy courses of earth to the end of the trail of the golden star, where the Wise Men bent on the voyage of discovery made the great Discovery of God. These wise, learned and mighty men, kneeling in pontifical robes upon a bedding of straw, before a Babe who could neither ask nor answer questions, offered their gifts and themselves as pledges of the obedience of the world. Their gifts were three: gold, frankincense and myrrh — gold, because He would rule as a king; frankincense, because He would live as a priest; and myrrh, because He would die like a man. At last the Wise Men had discovered Wisdom.

Only the shepherds and the Wise Men found Christ, but think of the thousands who did not. The world in those days, as in our own, was full of the worldly wise, but none of them discovered God. There was many an agnostic in Rome telling a young Pilate that there is no such thing as truth; there was many a sophist in the market place of Athens teaching that man could dispense with the gods; there were vain poets glorifying license under the name of liberty, and injustice in the name of progress; but to none of these souls did there come the vision of an angel or the light of a star. And *why?* Because the treasures of wisdom and knowledge, of healing grace and salvation, are reserved only for the extremes, in the intellectual order as well as in the moral. When God was a Babe only the intellectual extremes of simplicity and wisdom found their way to the crib; when God was a Man only the moral extremes of sinfulness and innocence found their way to His feet.

The innocent, like John, came to Him because they did not need to be cleansed; the sinners, like Magdalene, came to Him because they felt the need of being cleansed. But that middle group of Pharisees, who reprimanded His Apostles because they did not wash their hands before eating, hypocrites who were like whitened sepulchers, outside clean but inside full of dead men's bones; the self-righteous, who were half depraved and half intact, who were never hot with love nor cold with hate, these never knelt before the uplifted hand of the Sacred Heart. They are the kind that Scripture says shall be vomited from the very mouth of God.

As the arches of the centuries mark the pathway of history, the crib became the Church which Our Blessed Lord grounded upon Peter. The remarkable thing is that the same two classes of people who found their way to the crib find their way to the Church. Only the heirs of the shepherds and the descendants of the Wise Men ever enter its sacred portals. This is just another way of saying that the Church has room only for two extremes: those who think, and those who do not think, but it has no room for those who think that they think.

The Church is found first by the simple or

those who do not think — that great mass of men and women whose ignorance is more illumined than the doctrines of learned men — simple souls who because of their ordinary routine labors, like shepherds on Judean hills, have no time for learned study, or who, if they do have time, prefer, like those same shepherds, to be instructed by the angels or the ambassadors of God. For this great army which does not think, there is the authority of the Church, which they accept with the same loving obedience with which a child accepts the dictates of its parents. They do not want to know why the Church calls the eternal birth of the Second Person of the Trinity a generation, and the procession of the Third Person aspiration; they do not want to know how the accidents of bread and wine can exist without the substance of bread and wine, any more than a child wants to know the details of the city government under which his parents vote. They want only to know *what* the Church teaches — that is enough. They want only to know what the Vicar of Christ says — this satisfies them. The world calls them fools and says the Church is filled with the ignorant. Yes, the Church is filled with millions of simple souls who obey authority for no other reason than because it is authority; but that does not mean they are fools. It only means that the Church, like the cave of Bethlehem, is filled with simple shepherds.

But the Church takes care not only of those

who do not think, but also of those who do think: and by those who think I mean the profound and the real seekers after truth. From the days of the learned Paul down to our own, the Church has had to take care of the learned, the profound, and the Wise Men. There have been those who wanted to know not only the authority of the Church, but the reason behind authority; not only that the Church is infallible, but why the Church is infallible; not only that there are three Persons in the Blessed Trinity, but why there are not four. The Church has to take care of them, as the crib had to husband the Magi, and to those minds who would drink deep of the Pierian spring, who would take soundings of the Infinite, and would search with the telescope of faith those unexplored regions of thought which the eye of reason can not attain, the Church throws open the deep wells of philosophy and theology, in comparison to which all our higher mathematics and astral physics are but the shallow streams of the prairies and the playthings of the human mind. The world says that such learning of the Church is vain; that its theology is not profound; indeed, that it is foolish! But that does not mean it is foolish. It only means that the Church, like the cave of Bethlehem, is filled by Wise Men who were vain enough to follow a star until it led to God.

But between the extremes of the simple souls who live by faith, and who are content to be children all their spiritual lives, and the learned souls like Augustine and Aquinas whose torches of wisdom, lit at the foot of the crucifix, continue to illumine a darkened world — between these extremes there is no mean. The simple shepherds heard the voice of an angel and found their Lamb; the Wise Men saw the light of a star, and found their Light. But Herod the Great, who lived within a dozen miles of the shepherds and was visited by the Wise Men en route to the crib, never found God — not even in his massacre.

All the race of proud Herods from that day to this, who think that they think, have missed God either because they are too complicated to understand the simple reports of the shepherds, or too filled with useless learning to grasp the only useful truth which the Wise Men bring. They lack that quality which the modern world conspicuously lacks, namely, teachableness or what the Latins called docility. Therefore they disdain the idea that God might add to their knowledge by revelation. Some of them, to cover up their pride, go so far as to attack the Church as something antiquated and behind the times. They really should be denied the privilege of attack and criticism, because they never earned the intellectual right to do so — they do not know anything about the Church.

And so I repeat what I said at the beginning that humility, which is common to the simple and the wise, is the condition of discovering Wisdom. If our age lacks any quality at all, it is what might be called teachableness, or what the Latins called docility. Minds today rely principally on what they have obtained by their own thought or reading. Some fancy they can find out truth entirely by themselves and disdain the idea that God might add to their knowledge by revelation. Others believe that Wisdom is synonymous with a smattering of facts about science, or the book of the month, or the new skull dug up in Peking. Even university education has become so impregnated with the research of useless facts, that it forgets research is only a means to an end, which is the discovery of Truth. It is well to remember that Herod is what many of our universities would have called a man of research, for he inquired diligently where the Child was to be born. But the Wise Men understood education far better. They were men of research too, for they searched the skies — but they were humble enough to know that research was only an instrument, and so they followed their science of the stars until it brought them to the Wisdom who made the stars, Jesus Christ our Lord.

Only the teachable find the Teacher, only the docile find the Doctor, only the humble find the Exalted. The simple souls, such as shepherds, find God because they know they know nothing; the really learned souls, like the Wise Men, find God because they know they do not know everything. And from that day to this the great mass of converts to the Church is made up of simple souls like the poor old woman who wanted to be a Catholic because she would like to say her beads before Our Lord in the tabernacle, and the really learned souls like Chesterton, Lunn, Belloc, Maritain, who know so much history, philosophy, and literature that they could not stay away from the Church, once the grace of God was given them. That too is why God sends into each age of history the saint conspicuous for the virtue the world needs most. And so in these days of pride, and self-conceit, He raised up the Little Flower, who, although possessed of the Wisdom that saves, was as simple as a child, and who although living in a day when men judged power by the great things they could raise up on earth, rather judged power by the roses she would let fall from Heaven. Through her intercession hundreds of thousands of converts have been brought to the Wisdom of the Crib and the Strength of the Cross. The extremes of simplicity and learning meet in the Church. Through her the ignorant peasant and the university professor find a common ground: they know what each must believe. Thus the Church may be defined as a place where we can stand responsible for one another's opinions. The learned know what the simple must believe, and the simple know what the learned must believe, namely, that there is no other name under Heaven given to men whereby they may be saved, than the name of the Babe in the Crib. But the Herods of the world never find the Church as they never find Christ — not even in their attempt to slaughter it; and the reason is that men never feel a tug toward the Church until they have ceased to pull against it. They must treat it with an open mind —even when they fear that it may be right — but that is just another way again of saying we must be humble.

Our Lord was not born under an open sky, under which men might walk erect, but in a cave, the entrance to which can be gained only by stooping. The stoop is the stoop of humility. Some minds are too proud to stoop, and so they miss the Joy that is inside the cave. The shepherds and Wise Men were humble enough to stoop, and when they stooped they found they were not in a cave at all, but in another world where there lived a beautiful woman with the sun above her head, the moon beneath her feet, and in her arms the Babe in whose tiny fingers was poised the very earth in which we live. And as shepherds and Wise Men knelt in adoration, I wonder whether the wise envied the simple, or the simple envied the wise. I believe the Wise Men envied the shepherds, because their way was quicker — they were not so long in discovering the Wisdom, which is God.

THE ARTISAN OF NAZARETH

III

THE ARTISAN OF NAZARETH

I N THE PAST MAN TALKED LESS about living his life, and more about saving his soul. But in our age the emphasis has shifted from the religious and the moral to the political and the economic. The attraction toward Heaven has decreased, and the gravitation toward the earth increased. The single quest for God has given way to the double quest for power and wealth. The modern man, isolated from God and uprooted from the great spiritual patrimony of the ages, craves to satisfy the egotism of his mind by commanding, and the egotism of his body by enjoying. Hence the successful man of our day is the man who has power and the man who has wealth.

But running counter to these modern ideals is a double force seeking to destroy them: the force of Anarchy and the force of Bolshevism.[1] Anarchy contends that all power is wrong, and hence would

---

[1] A radical totalitarian form of socialism based on the dictatorship of the proletariat and the elimination of private property: Soviet Communism.

throw all governments into the dust. Bolshevism holds that all wealth is wrong, and hence would confiscate private fortunes to swell the coffers of the State.

In the face of these two extremes, the one glorifying power and wealth, and the other condemning them, the earnest soul seeks a sane solution. He asks himself such questions as these: Are power and wealth absolutely wrong? Is the Anarchist justified in condemning all power, and the Communist right in destroying all wealth?

There is only one yardstick by which these ideals may be measured, and that is by the life and doctrine of Him who walks across the modern stage as time shifts its scenery from Nazareth to New York, and from Genesareth to the Thames. The hidden life of Nazareth is the eternal answer to the problem, and the answer is that power and wealth are legitimate ambitions and ideals, but — and here Our Lord breaks with the modern world — but *no man has a right to power until he has first learned to obey, and no man has a right to wealth until he has first learned to be detached*. This is the double lesson of Nazareth contained in the only two simple facts we know about His hidden years: first, that He was subject in obedience to His parents; and secondly, that He was a poor village carpenter.

First, a word about power. Nazareth is not a trite story about the beauty of slavery and subjection, as some enemies of Christianity would have us believe. If Our Lord were merely a human child without any Divine prerogatives, then the carpenter shop might reveal a lesson that power was wrong. But obedience is only half the lesson of Nazareth. Our Lord was obedient; He was a servant; He was subject. But He was more than that! He was a Power who became obedient, a Master who became a servant, and a Lord who came not to be ministered unto but to minister. His power in the human order reached back through forty-two generations to Abraham, and in the Divine order to the eternal generation in the bosom of the Eternal Father; His power at birth was saluted by the harping symphonies of angelic glorias; His power at twelve confounded the wise doctors of the Temple as He unraveled to them the wisdom of a Son on the business of His Heavenly Father; His power at thirty made the unconscious waters blush into wine and the seething sea hush into calm, and His power at thirty-three reminded a Pontius Pilate about to execute his authority as governor and ruler that the real seat of his power was not in Rome, but in the heavens above. Yet He who had all this power and who said that to Him "all power is given in heaven and on earth," passed practically the whole of His life in a despised village and degraded valley, with no flash of outward pomp and circumstance, subject to a Virgin and a just man, whom He knew before they were made, and who after they were made were really His own children. What was all this but a lesson to the world which misunderstands power, either by glorifying it, or by overthrowing it: namely, that no man has a right to command until he has learned to serve, and no man has a right to be a master until he has learned to be a servant, and no man has a right to power until he has learned to be obedient.

Why has so much of the power in the history of the world degenerated into tyranny? Why has so much of the authority of governments in the history of the world corrupted into force? It is because those who had power did not know how to obey, and those who had authority did not know how to be subject. Now if those who have power, whether it be the heads of governments, the leaders of nations, or the masters of political influence, recognize no power above them whose laws they must obey and whose judgment they must fear, then where shall they learn that obedience without which no man can justly govern? If there be no King of Kings, then what shall stay power from degenerating into tyranny? What was Pilate but the power of Rome, without the obedience of Nazareth? What is social snobbery, but royal birth without Nazarene simplicity? What is pride, but a Palm Sunday without the sobering prelude of a carpenter's shop? Our Lord came into this world not to condemn power: power there must be, authority there must be. For what is power but the Law of God in the hearts of men, as well as in the kernel of the seed? Our Lord did not come to take away power. He came to teach us how to use it. He came to tell us that *no man shall exercise his power in the pomp of Jerusalem, until he has learned to serve in the servitude of Nazareth*; that no man shall be a general until he has learned how to serve in the ranks, and that no one shall be a Lord until he has learned to be unlordly. Salvation in a world crisis lies, therefore, not in revolutionary attempts to upset governments, nor in the anarchist's attempt to subvert authority, nor in the demagogic democracy which would suffer no other head to mount above one's own — rather does salvation lie in all powers, political, social and economic, becoming subject to a power above them. If they do this, then they can say they are entitled to obedience because they are obedient to the power above them; then they can say they must be respected as an authority, because they have learned to obey their Author; then they can say they must be reverenced, because they are reverent to their God.

Nazareth has yet another lesson to teach, and that is that *no one is entitled to wealth until he has learned to be detached*. In other words, Nazareth is not just a simple glorification of poverty, a fatalistic resignation to squalor, a calm indifference about hardship and hunger. Neither is it a condemnation of wealth. In Nazareth Our Lord was poor; He was a needy village carpenter; He worked for the mere necessities of life. But He was more than that! He was not just a poor Man. He was a rich Man who became poor, just as He was a powerful Man who became obedient. His wealth was the treasure of Heaven which rust does not eat, moths consume, nor thieves break through and steal. His wealth was the wealth, not of a carpenter of Nazareth, but the wealth of a Carpenter who made the universe with its canopy of glittering stars and its carpet of lilies which toil not, neither do they spin. His wealth was the mansions of His Father's house which He had seen, but the beauty of which the human eye has never seen, nor the ear heard, nor the heart of man conceived. Yet, with all the wealth of God, He became poor; for He chose to be born in a shepherd's cave, work as a tradesman, preach as a vagabond, with nowhere to lay His Head, die on a poor man's cross, and be buried in a stranger's grave. The world before had heard of wealthy men giving away their wealth to be philanthropists.

The world had heard Buddha ask his disciples to renounce wealth, had seen Crates of Thebes give his gold to the poor, and heard the Stoics eulogize poverty at rich banquets; but the world before had never heard of poverty being not an ascetic rule, not a proud disguise for ostentation, not a philosophical ornament nor a mystic mood, but a step to higher perfection which is union with the Spirit of God. Others had said, "Sell all you have"; but only He added, "Then come follow Me." His life and doctrine are not those of many of our social reformers who, seeing the abuses of wealth and the excesses of capitalism, provoke class conflict and demand the division of wealth even though it was honestly earned. Those who would harangue the rich find no support in the simple Nazarene. *No one has a right to despise the rich until like Our Blessed Lord he has proved he is free from the passion of wealth.* That is why He could be as hard on the selfish rich and say to them that it was easier for a camel to pass through the eye of a needle than for a rich man to enter the Kingdom of Heaven. The poverty of Nazareth was not a condemnation of wealth; neither was it a glorification of wealth; neither was it a canonization of poverty as such. It was the preachment of the beautiful doctrine of detachment, by which men free themselves from the passion of wealth for the glory of God and the salvation of souls — even though that wealth is only their own will and a few fishing boats and tangled nets.

Why has so much of the wealth of the world ended in wars over wealth? Why have so many of the rich been greedy, and so many of the wealthy been misers? Why have so many of the poor been bitter and so many of the wealthy unhappy?

It is because they do not know what it means

to be detached. It is because they never learned the lesson of Nazareth, which is to have all things and possess nothing. If they understood Nazareth aright, there would be no occasion for saying with Professor Joad of Cambridge University that God is cheaper than a living wage and the governing classes have found it expedient to exploit Him to the utmost.

Our Lord never sought to keep the poor satisfied with their poverty, nor the miserable satisfied with their misery, just because they were poor or because they were miserable. He glorified not the poor man, not the rich man, but the poor man who was not always poor; the poor man who once was rich; the poor man who by the law of detachment possessed everything, because he desired nothing; the poor man who became poor, not by giving away his wealth, but by exchanging it for the incommensurable riches of Heaven. And all this is only another way of saying, not "Blessed are the rich," nor "Blessed are the poor," but "Blessed are the poor in spirit."

When He who was rich became so poor that He could state: "The foxes have their holes, the birds of the sky have their nests, but the Son of Man has nowhere to lay His head" (Lk 9:57); and when He to whom all power was given in Heaven and earth, girded Himself with a towel and on the night before He died humbled Himself by washing the feet of His own Apostles, He taught us how to be poor without being Communists and how to be obedient without being revolutionists. He reminded us that poverty and slavery no more entitle a man to the Kingdom of Heaven than do wealth and power, but that the rich man would enter Heaven if he would be poor in spirit and the powerful masters would enter Heaven if following His example in the Upper Room they would act as the servants of God. The carpenter's shop therefore is not a truism about the beauty of poverty and the holiness of slavery. It is a paradox about the richness of the poor in spirit, and the power of the masters who serve. As a matter of fact Our Blessed Lord is the only One who ever walked this dreary earth of ours of whom the rich and the poor, the masters and the servants, the powerful and the slaves, could say: *He came from our ranks! He is one of our own!*

THE WAR WITH TEMPTATION

IV

The War With Temptation

T HE GREAT CHARACTERISTIC of our age is not its love of religion, but its love of talking about religion. Even those who would smite God from the heavens make a religion out of this irreligion, and a faith out of their doubt. On all sides — from a thousand pens, a hundred microphones, scores of university rostrums — we have heard it repeated, until our very head reels, that the "acids of modernity" have eaten away the old faith and the old morality, and that the modern man must have a new religion to suit the new spirit of the age.

This new religion, we are told, must be absolutely different from anything that ever existed before. It must be just as fresh and modern as the brilliant age in which we live, with its new hopes, new visions, and new dreams. When we inquire diligently into the characteristics of this new religion, we are told it must be social, it must be political, it must be worldly.

By social they mean it must dedicate itself, not

to the illusory pursuit of the spirit, but to the practical needs of the body. The religious man of the new era will be the one who gives bread to hungry stomachs, clothes to naked backs, and roofs to unsheltered heads. Better milk for babies, better playgrounds for children, better bread for the poor — these, and not faith, grace, and sacraments, are the things on which man lives; and that religion which gives these social necessities is the religion of the future.

Next, we are told that the new religion must be political, and by that is meant that it should cease talking about the Kingdom of God and begin talking about the republics of earth. All its energies and zeal must be directed to support governmental policies such as liquor control, gold standards, and labor codes; there must be a swing away from the stress on eternity, prayers, and the communion of saints; for the world problems, in need of a solution, are not religious, we are told, but economic and political.

The final characteristic of the new cult will be its worldliness. Too long has religion emphasized responsibility to God and dwelt on duties to Him, instead of service to our fellowmen. The new religion has no time for the thought of responsibility to God, for "the modern man," George Bernard Shaw tells us, "is too busy to think about his sins." It makes man the master of all he surveys, the lord of his own life, and, therefore, one who may shuffle off by his own hand if he chooses; for who is there who will dare say Nay?

Now let us ask the new prophets: How old is their new religion? Is it really a new thing, or is it merely an old error with a new label? Let us go back two thousand years to the Eternal Galilean and learn not only that the new religion is just an old temptation, but also that resistance to it is the pledge and promise of Life Everlasting.

Go back to the picture of Our Blessed Lord as He stood in the untenanted wilderness which stretches southward from Jericho to the Dead Sea. There His forerunner John, with bronzed countenance, unshorn locks, leather girdle, and mantle of camel's hair, whose drink was the water of the river and whose food was locusts and wild honey, saw the heavens open and the Spirit of God descend in dove-like radiance over his Master's Head, as there rang out over the Jordan river, a voice which to unpurged ears was like thunder: "You are my beloved Son, in you I am well pleased" (Lk 3:22).

With the waters still dripping from His noble head, Our Lord went out into the solitude to put a desert between Himself and humanity. For forty years the Jewish people wandered in the desert before entering into the kingdom promised by God. For forty days Moses remained close to God to receive His law on tablets of stone. Now, before announcing His Kingdom, to which Moses and the chosen people had pointed, Our Blessed Savior retires for forty days into the lonely mountains, where no human face was to be seen and where no human voice was to be heard. After forty days of fasting, He was tempted by Satan. Tempted He could be, for He had taken the armor of human flesh, not for idleness, but for battle. Oh! Do not mock the Gospels and say there is no Satan. Evil is too real in the world to say that. Do not say the idea of Satan is dead and gone. Satan never gains so many cohorts, as when, in his shrewdness, he spreads the rumor that he is long since dead. Do not reject the Gospel because it says the Savior was tempted. Satan always tempts the pure — the others are already his. Satan stations more devils on monastery walls than in dens of iniquity, for the latter offer no resistance. Do not say it was absurd that Satan should appear to Our Lord, for Satan must always come close to the godly and the strong — the others succumb from a distance.

But in what did Satan tempt Christ? Here is the remarkable side of that temptation, and one which has such a bearing on our own day. Satan tempted Our Blessed Lord to preach another religion than that which He was about to preach. Our Lord was about to preach a divine religion. Satan tempted Him to preach a religion that was not divine, but a religion which the modern world calls *new*! In a word the three temptations of Satan against Christ are the three temptations of the world against the

Church today, namely, to make religion: social, political and worldly.

Satan first tempted Our Lord to make religion social: to make it center about the materialities of life, such as bread for starving bodies like His own. Pointing from the top of the mountain to the stones whose shapes resembled little loaves of bread, he said: "Tell these stones to become loaves of bread" (Mt 4:3). It was Satan's challenge to God to make religion center around the materialities of life. But the answer of Our Blessed Lord was immediate: "Not by bread alone shall man live, but by every utterance proceeding from the mouth of God" (Mt 4:4). By that response, Our Lord declared that religion is not social, in the sense that its primary function is to give food to the body, but rather divine, in the sense that it must give food to the soul. Men must have bread! There is no disputing that point. Our Lord taught us to ask the Father to "give us this day our daily bread"; He even went so far, when men were in dire need of it in the desert places, to multiply bread even to excess. But beyond that, He told the thousands at Capernaum, He would not go. "You seek me... because you ate of the loaves and were satisfied. Labor not for food that perishes, but for food that remains for life eternal" (Jn 6:26-27). Religion is not purely social. If salvation were only economic relief, if religion were only to give bread to hungry stomachs, then dogs would be invited to its banquet. No! Man has a higher principle than that of the beasts, and a higher life than that of the body. We come into this world not just to sit and rest, to work and play, to eat and drink. Hence, that religion which would make the securing of bread its chief object in life, and would seek no divine food, will starve with hunger in the midst of plenty. There must come dark hours when God must be trusted, even in hunger. There must even come moments in starvation when bread must be refused, if it means the sacrificing of a principle that endangers the soul.

It is no justification to say we must live, because bodily life in itself is not necessarily the best thing for us. It is better for us not to live, if we cannot live without sin. For it is never right for us to starve our spiritual nature to get bread for our bodies. Sometimes the best thing that we can do with our life is to lose it; and the best thing we can do with our body is not to fear those who would kill it, but rather to fear those who would cast our soul into hell. Religion need not neglect sociology; the priest at the communion rail need not forget the bread lines; the minister in the sanctuary need not forget the playgrounds. The earthly, the human and the social, are part of religion, but not the primary part, as Satan would have us believe. Rather, in searching for higher things, do we find the lower: "First seek the Kingdom and the will of God, and all those things will be given to you besides" (Mt 6:33).

Satan next tempted Our Lord to make religion political by exchanging the Kingdom of God for the kingdoms of earth. "Then [the Devil]... showed Him all the kingdoms of the world in an instant of time. And he said to Him: 'I can give you all this power and glory because it has been given to me and to whomever I want to give them. So, if you'll worship me, it will all be yours.' And in answer Jesus said to him: 'It is written: *The Lord your God shall you worship, and Him alone shall you adore*'" (Lk 4:5-8). By this answer Our Lord declared to all future ages that religion is not politics, that patriotism is not the highest virtue, that nationalism is not the highest worship, that the State is not the highest good. Devotion to the State there must be; loyalties to the kingdoms of earth there must be; tribute to Caesar there must be. Man is social, and living in society he must govern and be governed; he must be a patriot not only by supporting the just policies of those who rule, but even to the extent of laying down his life in just warfare for the common good. These things are self-evident. But Satan would have Christ adore the kingdoms of earth, convert the pulpit into a platform, and the Gospel into a national anthem. Our Lord would have us know that earthly kingdoms are but scaffoldings to the Kingdom of Heaven, that patriotism towards country is but the nursery to the adoration of God, and that it profits us nothing if we gain the whole world and lose our immortal soul.

Politics and religion are related something like the body and the soul. Both have their rights and their duties, but one is superior to the other. The primary concern of religion is not the rehabilitation of the kingdoms of the earth or the support of economic policies, for Our Lord came not to restore the politics of the world but to make a new Kingdom which needs neither armies nor navies, soldiers nor monies, slaves nor judges, but only renewed and living souls. He did not say religion must not be concerned with social injustice or indifference to political graft. Our Lord loved His own country so deeply and warmly that, as the first Christian patriot, He wept over it. *But He also loved the Kingdom of Heaven so much more, that He was willing to be put to death by the very country that He loved.* While time endures, Satan will always tempt religion to be wholly political, but until the end of time the due order must be preserved: "Render, therefore, to Caesar, the things that are Caesar's; and to God, the things that are God's" (Mt 22:21).

Satan's last assault was an effort to make religion worldly. The Gospel tells us Satan "led Jesus to Jerusalem and set Him on the parapet of the Temple and said to Him: 'If you're the Son of God, throw yourself down from here, for it is written, *He will give His angels orders concerning you, to protect you*; and, *On their hands they will carry you lest you strike your foot against a stone.*' In answer Jesus said to him: 'It is said: *You shall not tempt the Lord your God*"' (Lk 4:9-12). What a lesson is hidden in that answer for those who would make religion worldly, by emptying it of all responsibility and by making God merely a passive spectator of our falls and our suicides. The plea to cast Himself down from the pinnacle was not a sign of trust in God, but disbelief in God. It was an appeal, not to a natural appetite, but to a perverted pride which assumes that God is indifferent to our actions and disinterested in our decisions. The answer of Our Lord was a reminder that religion centers about responsible persons, and not about falling bodies; that man is endowed with free will and is therefore responsible for each of his actions down even to the least; that the universe in which he lives is moral, and therefore one in which we mount by making our dead selves stepping stones to higher things. That worldly religion which denies responsibility, sin, and judgment would reduce us all to mere stones falling from the giddy heights of stony pinnacles; it would make us merely material bodies obeying the law of gravitation which pulls us to the earth, instead of spiritual beings which, like fire, mount up beyond the stars to the Light of the World. Real religion does not say: "Throw yourself down," but "Lift yourself up"; for we are destined not to be stones of earth, but immortal children of God. Heaven and not the world is our final destiny. And so, instead of casting Himself down like a cheap and vulgar magician, Our Lord casts Satan down, and then goes out to another mountain top to give from its heights the Beatitudes of God, which lead to true beatitude with God in the everlasting glory of Heaven.

Thus the so-called new religion proves to be an old religion which Satan would establish on earth. There is no new birth in this new faith, but the same old spirit in the same old Adam, full of selfishness, envy, and sin. By vanquishing temptation, the Eternal Galilean has trumpeted to all nations and to all time the supreme truth that religion is not primarily social, nor political, nor worldly. Rather its function is to minister *divine life* to society, *divine justice* to politics, and *divine forgiveness* to the worldly. The world today is really seeking such a divine religion and is near starvation, as modern sects bring to it only the husks of humanism. The minds of today are beginning to see that our problems are not primarily economic and political, but religious and moral; that society will not and cannot be reformed from without, but only from within. It is only by the spirit of Christ and the spirit of prayer that the freedom of man, won by bloodshed and national sacrifice, can be safeguarded and preserved. The shattering of all our material illusions during the World War and during the present economic recession has made the clear-visioned minds of our day see that apostasy from the principles of the Savior, the abandonment of the spiritual life, and the transgression of the commandments of God, have led of necessity to our ruin and confusion worse confounded.

There is hope for us, however — and a glorious hope it is — in the victory of Christ over Satan. By permitting the Prince of Darkness to tempt Him, even though it was wholly exterior and did not touch His sinless soul, He proved that He is not insensible to our difficulties, our sorrows, and our temptations. We cannot say to Him what Satan said to God about Job: "But now put forth Your hand and touch his bone and his flesh, and surely You shall see that he will blaspheme You to Your face" (Job 2:5). Our Lord does know what it is to be tempted away from divinity and the primacy of the spirit; His bones, His flesh were touched unto scourging and crucifixion, and His answer was greater than Job's. Job answered: "The Lord gave and the Lord has taken away; blessed be the name of the Lord" (Job 1:21). But the Savior answered: "Not My will, but Yours be done" (Lk 22:42). Our King then is One who knows what it is to have His armor assailed by temptation for, in the language of Paul: "For our High Priest isn't One who is unable to sympathize with our weaknesses; He was tempted in every way we are, yet never sinned. Therefore, let us confidently approach the throne of grace to receive mercy and find grace to help us in time of need" (Heb 4:15-16). In Him we will find One who feeds us not on earthly bread which perishes, but on the heavenly manna which endures unto life everlasting; in Him we find One who vanquishes Satan, who would have us exchange an immortal soul for the perishable cities of the world; in Him we find One who asks us, not Satan-like, to cast ourselves down as stones from temples, but to lift ourselves up as souls into Heaven. He was born to change the world, to make its religion unworldly, its worship divine, and its food the Eucharist. He lived to teach us that life is a struggle, and that only those who persevere unto the end shall be saved. He was tempted in order to remind us that, as there was a flash of archangelic spears when His Father closed the gates of Heaven on the back of Satan, so shall there be a flash of spears and arrows of Heaven-directed prayer as His Church closes the gates of earth upon him who would make himself like unto God; for Christ, the King, the Savior, was born, lived, died, and rose to drive Satan from earth as His Father had driven him from Heaven.

THE WAY, THE TRUTH,
AND THE LIFE

V

The Way, The Truth, and The Life

T HERE IS A GENERAL TENDENCY in our day to frown
upon those who believe that Our Blessed Lord
is different from other religious leaders and reformers. It is even considered a work of intelligence to
rank Him along with the founders of world religions. Hence it is not uncommon to hear one who
prides himself on his broad-mindedness — which
gives offense to no religion, and a defense of none —
fling out a phrase in which Buddha, Confucius, Lao-
tsze, Socrates, and Christ are all mentioned in one
and the same breath; as if Our Lord were just
another religious teacher instead of religion itself.
Simply because a few resemblances are found between Our Lord and a few religious teachers, it is
assumed that they are all alike, that there is nothing
Divine about Christ. This is just like saying that
because most of the pictures in the Louvre are red,
green, white, and blue, that they were all painted by
the same artist.

It is my purpose to prove that Our Blessed

Lord is unique in the religious history of the world, and as different from all other teachers and reformers as God is different from man. This can be done, first, by considering three important revelations in His life: at Nazareth, where He said He was the Way; at Jerusalem, where He said He was the Truth; and at Capernaum, where He said He was the Life. And secondly, by contrasting them with the sayings of all religious teachers whoever they be.

The first scene is in Nazareth, which is a kind of backwater, a nowhere, a hermitage off the beaten track of life, where seemingly no man would live who loved the world and whose ambition rose above that of a village carpenter or a tiller of the soil. To that city, which is called "His own city," and which nestles in a cup of hills, Our Blessed Lord returned shortly after the opening of His public life. It was only natural that one of the first important declarations would be made to His own beloved townspeople, where His Sacred Heart had tabernacled Itself for almost thirty years. It was a Sabbath when He made His way across the town to the synagogue. His reputation had gone before Him, for it was generally known that He had worked a miracle at Cana and that He had gathered certain followers about Him at the Jordan and a few more at Capernaum. When every one assembled in the synagogue, the chazzan, or clerk, whose duty it was to keep the sacred books, drew aside the silk curtain of the painted ark which contained the manuscripts and handed Him the megillah, or roll of the Prophet Isaiah. Our Lord unrolled the scroll at the well-known sixty-first chapter which foretold the great Day of Mercy when One sent by God would fathom the depths of contrition, break the chains of the slavery of sin, and bring solace to a wounded world. In slow, clear tones which thrilled the hearts of every one in the synagogue that memorable Sabbath morning He read:

> The Spirit of the Lord is upon me,
> because He has anointed me:
> He has sent me to bring glad tidings to the
>   lowly,
> to heal the brokenhearted,
> To proclaim liberty to the captives
> and release to prisoners,
> To announce a year of favor from the Lord
> and a day of vindication by our God
>
> (Is 61:1-2).

He stopped reading and restored the scroll to the chazzan. A moment of silence followed, which seemed like an eternity. The silence was broken as the Eternal seemed to step out of His eternity and let ring out over that little group of His townsmen the fulfillment of the prophecy of Isaiah: "Today this Scripture has been fulfilled in your hearing" (Lk 4:21).

For the moment they did not catch the full import of His words. Then it dawned upon them that the most precious tradition and hope of their people was verified; that the Messiah for Whom they had yearned these four thousand years was now standing before them; that He was the One to whom Isaiah pointed seven hundred years before to proclaim the acceptable year of the Lord; that all that the kings, prophets, and judges of the past had written about the Nazarene who was to come, that all the heartfelt longing David sung on his lyre, were now fulfilled in their ears on this very day: for He was the One in Whom all Scriptures were fulfilled: He was the Expected of the Nations: He was Emmanuel: He was the unique Way of Salvation: He was God with us.

It was not just eloquence to which they were listening; it was something more; it was Truth uttering Itself, convincing by its own transparency, conquering them by the brilliance of its light and compelling them in their own heart of hearts to admit that behind it went an authority which compelled many to say, "Never did a man speak like that" (Jn 7:46). There was admiration in their minds, resolution in their wills, love in their hearts, and tears in their eyes, as they woke from their trance and began to speak.

When Our Blessed Lord sat down, it was like the dropping of a stage curtain which suddenly throws us back to ourselves and away from the drama which but a moment before absorbed our every thought. Now as they looked at one another, their old tones revived. Instead of thinking of Him as the unique Way of Salvation, they remembered Him as a poor carpenter just around the corner from the synagogue. For the village to submit to such a Man, for the elders to be taught by a carpenter, was not to be endured. A prophet is without honor in his own country. On one side were His own words that He was the Way, on the other side was the fact that He was one of their own; and the remark passed from mouth to mouth, "Isn't this Joseph's son?" (Lk 4:22).

A cry of execration rose up and filled the synagogue, a protest against His intolerance, a cry against His narrow-mindedness, a complaint against His assertiveness, and even His blasphemy for saying that He was the Way of God. In their excitement they rushed at Him, hustled Him out of the synagogue and into the street of the bazaar outside. With time, their fury gathered strength. They hurried Him down through the village, past the door in which thirty years before His Mother had received the word of an angel, round the curve of the valley below the town and up the gentle slope which ends abruptly over the Valley of Esdraelon. Not only should He be driven through the village, He should be thrown over the precipice beyond and meet the death that He deserved! They reached the peak of the mountain which drops precipitously like a yawning chasm at the far end of the village. They called to one another to push Him over, but something strange had happened. Their cries of revolt seemed hollow. They looked at their Victim and no man who ever saw Him ever forgot it to his last hour. As if they were smitten by God, the Nazarenes fled before the Nazarene. He left their city and never made His home there again. The wound had gone too deep. But in their eyes He had deserved death, because He claimed to be the very Way of God. And indeed He was the Way of God; for the Way of God is to slip from the fingers of men who would dare thrust Him over a rock.

The second scene is in the city of Jerusalem, during the Feast of the Tabernacles, which was at one and the same time a harvest festival and a commemoration of the journey of the Hebrews through the desert. As soon as Jesus appeared, He was sought out by the throng, for some were saying, "He's a good man," and others said, "No! On the contrary, he's leading the people astray" (Jn 7:12). At any rate the crowd felt they had a right to ask Him for His credentials. With a wonderful leap into the Infinite and Eternal. He declared to them that His doctrine is the very doctrine of God who sent Him and whose Eternal Son He is. The evening came and found Him seated in the court of the women, which contained the thirteen chests into which the people cast their gifts. In this court, and therefore very close to Him, probably on either side of Him, were two gigantic candelabra, fifty cubits high and sumptuously gilded, on the summit of which lamps were lit which shed their soft light over the Temple. Around these lamps the people in their joyful enthusiasm, and even the stateliest Pharisees, joined in festal dances, while to the sound of flutes, the Levites on the fifteen steps which led to the court, chanted the beautiful psalms which were known as the "Songs of Degrees." As Our Lord sat between those two great lights which illumined the kindly faces of friends and the sinister faces of enemies, they seemed to shine upon Him as on no one else, throwing a beautiful golden aureole about His majestic Head. It was His constant plan to shape the illustrations of His discourses by those external incidents which would fix the words most indelibly on the minds of His hearers. Just as before He had given the parable of the vineyard as He stood near a vineyard, and the parable of the fisherman as He talked to fishermen at the lake, so now did He declare His mission to the world as He stood in the light of those candles. In the color of their imagery, in the flaming brilliance of their light, on the very threshold of the Holy of Holies, the Holy of Holies proclaimed that the Light of God had come to the darkness of men:

> "I am the Light of the world.
> Whoever follows me will not walk in darkness,
> But will have the light of life" (Jn 8:12).

There was no mistaking His words. He did not say He was like a light; He did not say He was something like those candles now illumining the darkness; He did not say that He was the Light of any particular people, but the very Light which is identical with Truth and which illumines every man coming into the world. To make such a statement He had to know all things. To their memory, in none of the great schools of Jerusalem had He ever learned, nor did He ever sit at the feet of their great Gamaliel. And so His auditors turned to one another saying: "How does this man know, having never learned?" And when they asked Him: "Who are you?", they were stunned with the declaration that He whose Truth was the Light of the world possessed it from all eternity. "Jesus said to them: 'I am not of this world... If you abide in my word, you're truly disciples of mine, and you will know the truth and the truth will set you free'" (Jn 8:23, 31-32). His hearers, not grasping the great truth that He was the Light of the world, asked: "Are you greater than our father Abraham, who died?" (Jn 8:53). The response of Our Lord was an affirmation of His Eternity: "Your father Abraham rejoiced to see my day: he saw it and was glad." They therefore said to Him: "You're not fifty years old yet, and you've seen Abraham?" Jesus said to them: "Amen, amen, I say to you, before Abraham came to be, I am" (Jn 8:56-58).

"I am." Yahweh. It was terrific! This Man of

Nazareth now made Himself equal to Light, equal to Truth, equal to God. To be the son of Abraham was to be their Light; to be the Son of God was to be the Light of the world. It is Our Lord's battle-cry to an erring world, a tocsin[1] sounding to slaves about to be liberated in the name of the Truth which makes men free. But just as the midday sun is too strong for weak eyes, so the Light of the world was too brilliant for minds yet accustomed only to the candlelight. And so, in their fury against One Who claimed to be the unique Truth of the world, the Light of Life, and the Wisdom unborn in the agelessness of eternity, they picked up stones to throw at Him. But as their arms drew back for the sling, He had hidden Himself, proving once more that He was the Truth, for Truth always hides from those who seek to kill, and do not search in simplicity and humility of heart.

The third scene took place in the countryside of Capernaum. It was the day after He had fed five thousand who had followed Him into the desert, and from whom He hid, lest they make Him king. They had sought long for Him, and when at last they had found Him, on the other side of the sea, their first question was: "Rabbi, when did you come here?" (Jn 6:25). But Our Lord ignored their question, for that did not concern them. What did concern them was a proper understanding of the

---

[1] An alarm bell.

miracle He had worked for them when He gave them bread and fish. He knew they were slow to understand. He had pointed out to them that the more He did for them the more they looked upon Him as a material benefactor and would not see the greater spiritual things which were beyond. They were bent only on earthly life and kingdoms of this world. He would now make one last effort to bring them to an understanding of His mission: "Amen, amen, I say to you, you seek Me not because you saw signs, but because you ate of the loaves and were satisfied. Labor not for food that perishes, but for food which remains for life eternal which the Son of Man will give you, for God the Father has set His seal on Him" (Jn 6:26-27). So they said to Him, "Lord, give us this bread always." And Jesus answered: "*I* am the Bread of Life. Whoever comes to Me will not hunger, and whoever believes in Me will never thirst" (Jn 6:34-35). "I am the living Bread that came down from Heaven. Anyone who eats this Bread will live forever, but the Bread that *I'll* give for the life of the world is My flesh" (Jn 6:51). "Just as the living Father sent Me, and I live because of the Father, so too, whoever feeds on Me will live because of Me" (Jn 6:57). The last words were clear and emphatic. As He had before said that He was the Way and the Light, so now He was saying that He was the Life of the world. To believers and unbelievers alike it came as a shock. He was now identifying Himself with Life as He had identified Himself with Truth. Impossible or not, He had said it. The old murmurs broke out again, not this time from the vulgar-minded mob but from His own disciples who were scandalized at His saying that He came down from Heaven and that His life was the life of the world.

Some of them murmured: "This teaching is hard; who can accept it?", and then left and walked with Him no more. They had understood Him aright, otherwise He would not have let them go.

The only ones who remained were those grouped around Peter, to whom Jesus said: "Do you, too, wish to turn back?"

Peter, the rock, answered: "Lord, to whom would we go? You have the words of Eternal Life, and we've believed and come to know that You're the Holy One of God" (Jn 6:60-67).

That was precisely the point. Since He is God He is our Life, for what is God but the Life of men? The identification was complete: His Person was Life. He came not to bring us life as a friend brings us bread. He is the Bread which is Life. And so on the night before He died, He did that which no one else on dying was ever able to do. Others leave their property, their wealth, their titles. But He on dying left His Life; for how can men live without Life which is God? Since the plant life which sustains animal life does not live on another planet but is near animal life, and since the animal life which sustains human life does not live in another universe but is near that which needs it, so in like manner shall the Divine Life which is the life of the soul be tabernacled among men in the Bread of Life and the Wine which cheers men's hearts (cf. Jg 9:13).

These three scenes and the great lesson in each were repeated the night before He died. Our Blessed Lord giving His last discourse to His followers was interrupted by Thomas asking: "How can we know the way?"

To which Jesus answered: "I am the Way, and the Truth, and the Life" (Jn 14:5-6).

Now go back to any other moral teacher the world has ever known and find a similar message. Take any of them, Buddha, Confucius, Lao-tsze, Socrates, Mohammed — it makes no difference which. Not one of them identified himself either with the Way of Salvation or with Truth or with Life. They all said: "I will point out the way"; but Our Lord said: "I am the Way." They all said: "I will tell you how to possess truth or how to discover light," but Our Lord said: "I am the Truth — I am the Light of the world." They all said, "I will help you attain undying life"; but Our Lord said: "I am the Life." Every reformer, every great thinker, every preacher of ethics in the history of the world pointed to an ideal outside himself. Our Lord did not. He pointed to Himself. Every founder of a world religion asked men to look to their systems, which was apart from their persons. Our Lord did not. He pointed to His person. Alcibiades, for example, asked Socrates what he should ask of the gods. Socrates told him "to wait for some greater teacher who would tell us how we were to conduct ourselves before God." Socrates did not say, "Look to me, I am the way." Rather, he said, "Look after me, and beyond me, and outside me." There was a distinction between the master and his system.

What is true of Socrates is equally true of Buddha. In the *Book of the Great Decease*, Ananda tries to obtain from Buddha when his end was near, direction and consolation. Buddha did not say, "Believe in me," or "Live by me," but answered, "Be a lamp unto yourself and a refuge unto yourself." He was practically saying "I am not the Light. I am not the Truth." It was something outside him. Confucius, the great reformer of the Orient, repeatedly disclaimed any special excellence in himself. "How dare I," he said, "rank myself with the sage and the man of perfect virtue?" He was practically saying, "The Life is not in me. These ideals are distinct from my historical existence." Even in the religion of Israel, the Hebrew prophets were moral teachers of their nation, who demanded without compromise obedience to the words spoken by them, but they claimed that their words demanded reverence, not because they were *their* words, but because they were the words of God. Hence the frequency of the expression in the Hebrew Prophets: "Thus says the Lord."

What is true of the past is true of the present. There is no reformer or preacher today who believes that he is the incarnation of the ideal. At best, most of them would say that they were signposts pointing to a heavenly Jerusalem, but in no case that they were the city itself.

It is in this that Christ differs from all of them. While Socrates was saying, "Wait for another," Christ was saying, "I am here. The Scriptures are fulfilled in your hearing." While Buddha refused to be a lamp to guide the poor dying Ananda, Christ was saying, "I am the Light of the world." While Confucius refused to see in himself a personification of his ideal of sinlessness, Christ was saying that He was Life and Resurrection. While the prophets of Israel pointed beyond themselves, Christ proclaimed Himself as the Expected One of the Nations.

There was, therefore, no Ideal outside His historical life. He is the Ideal. There was no system outside His Person. His Person is the system. There was no way apart from His Way, no Truth apart from His Truth, no life apart from His Life. There was nothing outside or beyond Him, for in Him all the scattered ways and truths and lives found their center and source, and to such an extent that He could dare assert that which no one else had ever dared assert: "Apart from Me you can do nothing"

(Jn 15:5). You may buy and sell without Me, you may enlarge your farms and construct your dwellings without Me, you may build your navies without Me, but you cannot take one step toward the Ideal, which is Divine Life, without Me, for I am that Life. You cannot even go to the Father without Me, for "the Father and I are One" (Jn 10:30).

Our hungry modern world needs to meditate deeply on this oneness of the ideal with the very Person of Christ. Since the middle of the nineteenth century human hearts have been trying to live on system: on Humanitarianism, the Religion of Modernism, the Religion of Science, the Religion of Humanism, the Religion of Beauty, Freudianism, Theosophism, Spiritualism, Idealism — on a thousand and one mixtures of musty rationalism, moldy superstition, worm-eaten necromancy, soured philanthropy, simian symbolism, which have made mysterious mystics out of men only for a passing hour. But these frozen abstractions cannot satisfy a heart, for a heart cannot live on a system about Truth, or a theory about Love, or a hypothesis about Life. The human heart can live only on love. There is only one thing a human heart can love — and that is a Person. Make that Person one with the Way to be followed, one with the Truth to be known, one with the Life to be lived, and that Way, that Truth, and that Life will pull at a thousand heartstrings, drawing from them the sweet symphony of love.

Such is the Person of Our Blessed Lord Who alone, of all men, combines the Ideal and the Historical in His own Person. Because He is the Ideal there is the romance of love about His Person; because He is an Historical Person there is the truth about that romance. Every one else told a romance. Our Lord lived it. Every one else was as trite as history. The Historical Christ was as romantic as love. The more deeply we think about the matter, the more we see that if God is good, we should look for His Way, His Truth, and His Life; not merely to be way, way up there in the heavens, but down here in the dust of our poor lives. After all, what have all people been hoping for at all times except an Ideal in the flesh? They could not go on dreaming dreams and painting symbols. The Jews looked forward to the Ideal in the flesh; the Gentiles, knowing not revelation, by their very idolatry were saying: "Well, if God will not come down to us to be Our Way, Our Truth, Our Life, then we shall make Him come down. We shall make His image in stone, in gold, and in silver." But the image could not satisfy any more than the systems of our day can satisfy. There was an abyss that only an Incarnation could cover. And so God did come down. He came down as the embodiment of our dreams — the flesh and blood of our hopes — the Romance of Love which is as true and real as history. That is why He is loved; that is why He is adored; that is why He is God. There is one title dear to all who find in Him the Way, the Truth, and the Life, a title which recognized His Divinity, which gives the creature a ready access to the Creator, the sinner an easy approach to the Holy, and our broken hearts an open door to the mending Love of the Divine; and this title which brings the Infinite to the human in most beautiful, loving, sweet familiarity is: *The Sacred Heart.*

THE LIGHT OF THE WORLD

VI

The Light of the World

THERE ARE THREE GREAT ROLES played by the Eternal Galilean, each of which is a revelation of His Divine Character: He is a Prophet or Teacher, a King or the Center of Hearts, and a Priest or the Redeemer of the World. The first of these roles, that of Teacher, we shall consider here, our purpose being to set in relief just how contradictory are the teaching methods of Our Lord and those of the world.

Only a God could use such unworldly methods and still be successful in impressing His message on all ages and all types of mind.

The world has always had prophets, but it was reserved for our day to be surfeited with them. Never before in history has there been so much thinking and so little coming to the knowledge of truth, so many schools and so little scholarship, so many wise men and so little wisdom, so much talking about religion and so little prayer. First of all, a word about the world as a teacher. There is no one point on which any of these teachers is agreed, there being as many opinions as there are heads. But there is great unanimity in the method of their teaching. All are agreed that a successful message must possess three qualities: it must be smart; it must be liberal; and it must be modern.

By smart, the world means the message must be sophisticated, so as to appeal to the intelligentsia and to frighten away the uninitiated. The modern prophet seeks to astound us with his outpouring of quaint scientific facts and to dazzle us with a deluge of high-sounding names in which sin is called a form of Oedipus Reflex, and religion is defined as a projection into the roaring loom of time, or a unified complex of psychical values; he hints at vast authorities in the background, dwells on prehistory rather than history; always tries to convince the man on the street, not how simple a truth is, but how complex.

Secondly, the twentieth-century prophets agree that the message must be liberal. By this is meant that it must reduce law to a few social virtues, substitute hygiene for morality, patriotism for piety, and sociology for religion. The ideal must never surpass an approximate justice approved by public opinion; there must be a minimum of restraint and inhibition, no mention of mortification, but endless repetition of catchwords such as "evolution," "progress," "relativity," and "service." In this way the message will attract the self-righteous, and at the same time not offend those who believe that ethics

must be suited to unethical lives, and morals to
unmoral ways of living.

Finally, the present-day prophet seeks not
only to be smart, but also to be modern. Above all
things else he wants to convince his hearers that his
doctrine is suited to the age; that we have outgrown
other codes of morals and religion; that, after all, we
do live in the twentieth century and not in the
thirteenth; that the primary reason why the world
should accept his teaching is not because it is true,
but because it is up-to-date.

Now turn back the pages of history to a Great
Prophet whose message has been more successful
than that of any teacher who ever lived. We discover
that His method was just the opposite. He upset all
worldly standards of teaching with the same beautiful serenity with which He overthrew the tables of
the money changers in the Temple. He did the very
things any other prophet would have called foolish.
He chose the very method the others labeled unsuc-
cessful. His teaching possessed the three opposite
characteristics of the world. He did not make His
message smart, but simple; not liberal, but transforming; not modern, but eternal.

In contrast with modern prophets the message
of Our Blessed Lord was not smart and sophisticated, but plain and simple. There is nowhere an
attempt to impress His auditors either with His
Omniscience or with their nescience. He is never

complex. There is no trick of rhetoric, no appeal to the intelligentsia, no pomp of demonstration, no monotonous deserts of laws and precepts such as are found in Buddha or Mohammed. On most occasions His sermons were given under the open sky, by the hillside, alongside the lake, or in the roadway. His words flowed as sweetly to single listeners as to enraptured crowds and could be caught up just as well by the learned inquirer in the lonely midnight, as by the frail woman at the noonday well. His phrases are taken out of common life and common experience which makes them plain to every age. His lessons were drawn from the very incidents of life before Him at the moment.

On one occasion, speaking to poor working-men on a street corner, He made use of their patched clothing, their old bottles and new wine, to bring home to them the truth of His Kingdom. On another, standing in the entrance to the Temple, ablaze with lights, and its pinnacles flaming torches, He said to His disciples: "I am the Light of the World" (Jn 8:12). One day on a hillside near the Lake of Galilee He saw on the opposite hill a man going out to sow his seed, and pointing His finger said: "Behold the sower went out to sow" (Mt 13:3); and as His disciples watched the man they heard the parable of the sower and his seed. He sees the fishermen gathering in their nets and calls them to be "Fishers of Men" (Lk 5:10). He sees a man, nicknames him

"Rock," and makes him the foundation upon which He builds His Church. He spoke of everyday joys and sorrows: of the salt on the table; of the village perched on the hill; of the candlestick on the window sill; of their sheep and their goats; their camels and the eyes of needles; their daily bickerings before the local judge, and their coarse language which He overheard on the street; the hot sun beating down on them; the lightning flash from east to west; the ditch over there between the fields; thorns and thistles; the sheep and wolves; the reeds shaken by the wind, and burning weeds; eggs and serpents; nets and fish; pearls and pieces of money; corn and oil; stewards and gardeners; kings and shepherds; the raven hovering above them; the daily wages hidden at home in moneybags; the cottage near the lake built on sand which had fallen to ruins, and the one built on rocks which survived the flood; courtiers in soft clothing, brides in nuptial robes, and the stones on the hillsides with snakes and scorpions beneath them.

And who shall ever forget the day that He stood on the plain, when His eye was first caught by the flight of a bird overhead, and then by a lily at His feet, which He took in His hand with the remark that it grows though it labors not, neither does it spin. Suddenly He elevates the minds of His hearers from that impotent flower to their national heroes and the flamboyant colors of their palaces: "Not even

Solomon in all his glory was arrayed as one of these" (Mt 6:26-29); and then finally, by a third thought, shrivels it to nothing with a gesture of one who might fling it away: "But if God so clothes the grass of the field, which is here today, and thrown into the oven tomorrow, won't He clothe you much better, O you of little faith?" (Mt 6:30). It was like building a great tower by magic and then suddenly crumbling it into dust when it had made us look up into the sky. There was nothing smart or sophisticated about it; it was a thing so simple that no worldly-minded person would ever think of it if he wished to impress us with his wisdom. Smart men say smart things to convince us of their smartness. It remained for a God to say simple things, to convince us of His Wisdom.

The second difference between the modern teacher and Our Lord is that the former believes that the message should be liberal, broad, and free from restraint and mortification. Our Blessed Lord said it should not be liberal. But in opposing a liberal doctrine He was not narrow; He was not revolutionary; He was not making an innovation. Rather He was renovating. His doctrine was transforming. He begins a recast race of Adam. Socrates reformed the mind, Moses the law, and others altered codes, systems, and religions; but Our Lord did not alter a part of man, but the whole man from top to bottom, the inner man which is the motive power of all His works and deeds. He therefore makes no compromises, or concessions. He has a real contempt of a broadmindedness which is synonymous with indifference. He tells us that if we do not believe, we shall be condemned, and that if we despise His ambassadors, we despise Him. Unprofitable servants are to be cast into utter darkness where there "shall be wailing and gnashing of teeth" (Mt 22:13); Sodom and Gomorrah shall be more tolerated on the Day of Judgment than the city which rejects the Apostles. Capernaum which was exalted to the heavens shall be thrust into hell. Add to all this His attacks on the Pharisees, which suggest anything but a gentle, liberal, broadminded enthusiast, too mild even to criticize his bitterest opponents: "Hypocrites... blind guides... whitewashed tombs... you serpents, brood of vipers: How will you escape being condemned to Gehenna?" (Mt 23:33).

Neither are there any inanities about loyalty — He never once used the word cooperation. There were no broad, inoffensive statements like "Leave life better than you find it"; or truisms such as the "Joy of Service," the "Gospel of Work," or "A Good Deed a Day." Rather He said that if the festival of happiness is ever to be celebrated again, we must be the opposite of what we are. We must conquer our animal instincts instead of satisfying them, pluck out our eye rather than let it scandalize us, cut off our hand rather than let it drag us into hell, refuse to answer fight with flight, which is fear, but show the enemy the other cheek and make a friend of him. We must not take thought of tomorrow for sufficient for the day is the evil thereof; we must not exalt but humble ourselves; we must rejoice when we are persecuted and bless when we are reviled; seek the lowest place at table; rejoice in the hatred of men, become simple like children; and above all take up a daily cross. Why? Because we were not born to wriggle in a worm heap, eating our particle of earth as if we had only a stomach and two hands; we must remember we have a heart and soul, the salvation of which is more important than the gaining of the whole world — "For what would it profit a man were he to gain the whole world and lose his soul in the process?" (Mk 8:36).

This ideal was new. No one before ever said it, because no one before ever came to transform the old Adam, which is nature, by creating a new nature, a supernature, made to the image and likeness of God. Every one else who ever lived told us how to reform the world; Our Lord told us how to reform ourselves. In a word He told us the world can be made better only by making ourselves better. Every one else told us how to make the road smoother. Our Lord told us to turn straight around and take a new road, to renounce what seemed good, pick up what had been thrown away, worship Him who was spurned, learn that which seemed foolish, crucify not our enemies but our lower selves, purge our hearts, hate hatred, love executioners, transform our souls, and answer the strong "No" of Christ to the foolish "Yes" of the world.

Because it was a transforming doctrine, it could be expressed only in paradoxes. Everything that humanity in its baser vision held dear, He set at naught; those things it sought He condemned; that which is put first He put last; that which is called death He called life. How express this turning upside down of human nature except in a paradox in which what is true for time is false for eternity, and what is good for the body is bad for the soul, and what is wisdom for the world is weakness with God? So there runs through this Preacher the tremendous paradoxes about the first being last, and the last first; that the humble shall be exalted and the exalted humbled; that by saving our life we lose it, and by losing our life we save it; that the scorned shall be reverenced, and the reverenced scorned; that the master shall be as the servant and the servant as the master; that tears shall be turned into joy, and those who laugh shall mourn; and above all that the harlots and publicans will enter the Kingdom of Heaven before the scribes and the Pharisees. These paradoxes constitute the only language in which God can talk to man, the Sinless to sinners, and the Eternal to the temporal. Man can talk to man in simple language without paradoxes; but when a God comes to this earth as man, to set at naught our cheap liberal morality, to create new values, to transform hearts by making them see how foolish the ways of men are to God, then He must speak on the two levels of time and eternity which is the language of paradox.

Finally, modern prophets, it was said, would rather be up-to-date than right, rather be wrong than behind the times. Our Blessed Lord upset this spirit by dwelling not on timely topics, but on eternal truths. He taught in such a manner as to disprove forever that His ideas were suited to His time, and therefore unsuitable to any other. He never used a phrase that made His philosophy dependent on the social order in which He lived; He never made His morality dependent on the exist-ence of the Roman Empire, or even the existence of the world: "Heaven and earth shall pass away, but My word shall not pass away" (Mt 5:18). He did not get His argument against divorce from the Mosaic Law, or the Roman Law, or Palestinian custom. It was an ideal outside time; difficult in all times; impossible at no times. Because He did not adapt Himself to past times, nor to present time, nor to future times, He never fell into a platitude. Plati-tudes belong only to those who say we must have new morals to suit the new science. Platitudes are the heritage of time, but not of the eternal. For example, there are no platitudes about war, about its waste, about its hate, about its slaughter. What there is, running through His teaching, is a little phrase which is a mighty phrase; a phrase which separates time from eternity, a phrase which began a new system of education: "But I say to you." In the Sermon on the Mount (Mt 5), He begins every example with the words, "You've heard it said…" and then He purifies the so-called timely, the platitudinous, with an eternal command: "But I say to you…." It recurs like an antiphon in His preaching. "You've heard that it was said to the ancients: You shall not kill…. But *I* say to you… whoever says, 'You fool!' shall be liable to the fire of Gehenna" (Mt 5:21-22). "You've heard that it was said, You shall not commit adultery! But *I* say to you, that anyone who looks at a woman with lust for her has already committed adultery with her in his heart" (Mt 5:27-28). "You've heard that it was said: An eye for an eye, and a tooth for a tooth. But *I* tell you not to resist the evildoer; on the contrary, if anyone strikes you on the right cheek, turn the other to him as well" (Mt 5:38-39). It was better according to His logic that the face should suffer rather than the soul. Enlarging the doctrine of charity, He gave a new law in which hate is transformed into love: "You've heard that it was said: Love your neighbor, and hate your enemy. But *I* say to you: Love your enemies, and pray for those who persecute you" (Mt 5:43-44). There is only one way of driving enemies from the earth, and that is by loving them.

There is nothing in any one of these statements which suited His times or suited any other times. The reason He was never concerned about being up-to-date was because He is beyond date, in the sense that He is outside time. Every one else who ever lived came from a certain people, and bore the imprint of his hour. How else could legislators govern unless their laws suited their times? How else could poets and philosophers write unless they had their finger on the pulse of their civilization?

In the rhythm of their poetry is the cry of their epoch; in the dreams of their philosophy is the aspiration of their century. Name the great ones of the earth: Homer, Job, Aeschylus, Isaiah, Socrates, Phidias, Sophocles, Plato, Virgil, Tacitus, Dante, Michelangelo, Shakespeare, Milton, Corneille, Bossuet, Washington, Lincoln. What are they but the incarnation of Greece, Arabia, Judea, Rome, Italy, Spain, France, England, and America? The greater they are, the more incarnate the genius of the humanity in whose hour they lived. The great Pelasgian is Homer, the great Greek is Aeschylus, the great Arab is Job, the great Hebrew is Isaiah, the great Roman is Tacitus, the great Italian is Dante, the great Frenchman is Bossuet, the great Englishman is Shakespeare, the great American is Washington. But who is Our Blessed Lord? He is neither Greek nor Roman, Jew nor Gentile, ancient nor modern. He is a man outside of time; the Man; the God-Man. In others you never find humanity in all its entirety, you touch only the hem of the garment; but in Christ you touch all humanity. This universality of Our Lord, this overflowing the limits of time and space, this peculiar property of belonging to all times because He belongs to no time — whence does it come? Whence that tremendous Personality? Whence the source of His independence? He depends not on the multitude who acclaim Him, not on the customs of His country, not on the century when He lived. If we are to find the secret of His Timelessness, the simplicity of His Wisdom, and the transforming power of His Doctrine, we must go out beyond time to the Timeless, beyond the complex to the Perfect, beyond change to the Changeless, out beyond the margent of the world to the Perfect God, who in the form of a humble Nazarene carpenter one day calmly and without emphasis, like one picking up a flower, looked over His shoulder and in one great and tremendous paradox revealed the secret of His ageless eternity in the strangest words this aging earth had ever heard: "Before Abraham came to be... I am."

THE KING OF HEARTS

VII

The King of Hearts

EVERY MAN IS PASSIONATELY fond of liberty, but there is one thing he craves even more, and without which existence and even liberty is painful, and that is happiness. It is one of the greatest of life's paradoxes that as much as man seeks to be free, he still wishes to be a slave: not a slave in the sense that his liberty is denied him, but in the sense that he yearns for something he can worship, something which will solicit his will, pull at his heartstrings, tempt his energies, and command his affections. He wants to be free to choose between the various kinds of happiness, but he does not want to be free from happiness. He wishes to be its slave.

There are two ways of responding to this soul hunger and this heart thirst. One is the way of the world, the other is the way of Christ. The difference between the two is that before we have the pleasures of the world they seem desirable and all that we need to make us happy. But after we have them, they are disappointing and sometimes even disgusting. The contrary is true of the pleasures of Christ. Before we have them they are hard, unattractive, and even repulsive. But after we have them they are satisfying, and all our heart could ever crave.

The problem then is this: Will the heart seek its happiness in the pleasures of the world, or will it seek them in the Kingship of Christ? I would plead for the Kingship of Christ, by showing in the language of Francis Thompson, first, how the pleasures of the world fail, and secondly how the Kingship of Christ pleases.

What kind of happiness is offered by the world? What solution does it give to the problem of joy? Happiness, says the world, is to be found in the pursuit of three things: Humanism, Sex, and Science.

The first panacea is Humanism, or the sufficiency of man without God. On this theory man finds satisfaction in his own mind without the aid of faith, and in his own will without the aid of grace. There is no need, according to this philosophy, to seek a God outside of man, but only the man inside himself, with his thoughts and imaginings. And the Humanist, in the language of Thompson, says the escape from God is in the joys of one's own mind, in psychology, in human emotions, in sentiments, in natural mysticisms. Through these it hopes to escape the call of the great King, Christ, and the sound of His Footfall of Peace.

I fled Him, down the nights and down the
      days;
  I fled Him, down the arches of the years;
I fled Him, down the labyrinthine ways
    Of my own mind: and in the midst of tears
I hid from Him, and under running laughter.
      Up vistaed hopes I sped;
      And shot, precipitated,
  Adown Titanic glooms of chasmèd fears,
From those strong feet that followed, followed
    after.[1]

And yet Humanism is not a success but a
failure, for man cannot live by himself, any more
than he can lift himself by his own bootstraps or live
on his own fat. He has a soul as well as a body, and
the spirit clamors for its food more unhesitatingly
than the stomach. As there floats over his soul the
truth that perhaps there is a God outside of and
beyond man, he hears the beat of the Feet of God
whom he was told he would never need:

    But with unhurrying chase,
    And unperturbèd pace,
  Deliberate speed, majestic instancy,
    They beat — and a Voice beat
    More instant than the Feet —
"All things betray thee, who betrayest Me."[2]

---

[1] Francis Thompson, *The Hound of Heaven.*
[2] *Ibid.*

Driven from self, the modern man next flies to the Freudian philosophy of Sex, opening the little casements of the heart, so narrow and tiny, which contrast with the great wide portals through which Divine Love enters. Influenced by the economic order in which he lives he begins to judge love like gold, and hence feels the more tempestuous and violent it is, the more real it is. He feels the need of religion, and since he would starve his soul, he makes a religion out of the instincts which he has in common with the beasts of the field. Pleading outlaw-wise, as one cut off from all human sympathy, he drinks of flesh, which makes hungry where most it satisfies. Somehow deep down in his heart, he knows that God is pursuing and will enter if He can; but his weak soul is afraid that if he admits the spirit he will have no room left for the flesh. Ah! so forgetful that if he has the Flame he can forget the spark.

> I pleaded, outlaw-wise,
> By many a hearted casement, curtained red,
>   Trellised with intertwining charities;
> (For, though I knew His love Who followèd,
>   Yet was I sore adread
> Lest, having Him, I must have naught beside.)
> But, if one little casement parted wide,
>   The gust of His approach would clash it to.
>   Fear wist not to evade, as Love wist to
>   pursue.[3]

---

[3] Ibid.

Finally the modern man, finding that Humanism and Sex both fail to satisfy, seeks his happiness in Science, as he becomes enthralled by the glory of the midday sun, the soft beauty of the moon, the splendor of a thousand stars. Since earth fails, he will play truant to earth, slip through the gate of fancy into the very meadows of the skies. The beauties of the planets dazzle him as he runs wild over the fields of ether. Science, it seems, is the only thing which will answer his call to happiness and be more than an echo dying on the winds. More than that it will explain the universe without that "tremendous Lover" who is God. And so he cries:

> Across the margent of the world I fled,
> And troubled the gold gateways of the stars,
> Smiting for shelter on their clangèd bars;

> * * *

> I said to Dawn: Be sudden — to Eve: Be soon;
> With thy young skiey blossoms heap me
> over
> From this tremendous Lover —

> * * *

> Drew the bolt of Nature's secrecies.
> I knew all the swift importings
> On the wilful face of skies;

> * * *

> I was heavy with the even,
> When she lit her glimmering tapers

> Round the day's dead sanctities.
>   I laughed in the morning's eyes.
> I triumphed and I saddened with all weather,
>   Heaven and I wept together,
> And its sweet tears were salt with mortal mine;
> Against the red throb of its sunset-heart
>   I laid my own to beat,
>   And share commingling heat.[4]

But Science fails too, for it is something more than a knowledge of matter the soul craves. There is no room for beauty in that science which would botanize even on a mother's grave. So the modern man, after wandering over the universe with a telescope in his hand, returns with bleeding feet and aching heart. The world has lied again! What it called a successful road to happiness was a failure. There wells up then from his heart the sad and painful truth that joy is not in nature:

> In vain my tears were wet on Heaven's grey
>   cheek.
> For ah! we know not what each other says,
>   These things and I; in sound I speak —
> Their sound is but their stir, they speak by
>   silences.
> Nature, poor stepdame, cannot slake my
>   drouth;

*   *   *

---

[4] *Ibid.*

Never did any milk of hers once bless
    My thirsting mouth.

*   *   *

I tempted all His servitors, but to find
My own betrayal in their constancy,
In faith to Him their fickleness to me.
    Their traitorous trueness, and their loyal
        deceit.
To all swift things for swiftness did I sue;
    Clung to the whistling mane of every wind.
    But …
Fear wist not to evade as Love wist to pursue.
    Still with unhurrying chase,
    And unperturbèd pace,
Deliberate speed, majestic instancy,
    Came on the following Feet,
    And a Voice above their beat —
"Naught shelters thee, who wilt not shelter
        Me."[5]

This story is relived in a thousand times ten thousand lives. The soul craves happiness. The world says: I have the successful secret. It is Humanism, it is Sex, it is Science. And yet all these fail! Humanism is too inhuman; sex is too remorseful; science is too cold.

Where then find happiness? Where find that one thing whose slave we love to be, and yet be free?

---

[5] *Ibid.*

Who is it who calls to us after each of our failures? "All things betray thee, who betrayest Me." Who is it who whispers to our heart after each sin? "Lo, naught contents thee who contents not Me." Where seek that haunting voice which seems to call to us from every burning bush of the foibles of earth?

May it not be that since the world does not give happiness, we must seek it in something unworldly? May it not be that since what the world called successful failed, we must seek the successful in what the world calls failure? But there is only one thing in all the world which is unworldly enough to be Divine; and only one thing which was a failure enough in the eyes of the world to be a success with God. That is the Person who brought to this old earth of ours a Love which cries out: "Come to Me, all you grown weary and burdened, and I will give you rest" (Mt 11:29). That is Christ the King.

But did He ever call Himself a King? Recall that terrible day which we call *Good* Friday, to mask its heinousness and to declare our *felix culpa*. Our Lord is led before the Roman Procurator in the name of Tiberius Caesar. To have some idea of Pilate's personality and his vision of the world worldly, make a mental picture of him in terms of one of our modern intelligentsia — a reader of Mencken, Bertrand Russell, and Shaw, with Swinburne and Wells on his bookshelves, one whose emotional life was dictated by Havelock Ellis and his mental life by Julian

Huxley, who says there is no such thing as truth. Standing between the pillars of his judgment seat, touched somewhat with the nobleness of the Divine Prisoner, Pilate asks with pitying wonder: "Are You a King?" (Jn 18:33). The very way he said it was meant to imply: Are You, whom the world receives not, who are a poor, worn outcast, in this the hour of Your bitter need — "are You a King"; are You, pale, lonely, friendless, wasted man in poor peasant garments and tied hands — "are You a King"; are You who fled when the crowd attempted to make You a worldly king, and who only last Sabbath entered the palm-strewn streets of this Holy City amidst pompous splendor — "are You really a King?" There came from that beaten figure, rising to its full stature, expressing kingship in every gesture despite ropes and chains: "You say that I am a king" (Jn 18:37). "My Kingdom is not of this world; if My Kingdom were of this world My attendants would fight so that I wouldn't be handed over to the Jews, but as it is My Kingdom is not from here" (Jn 18:36). "For this was I born, and for this I came into the world — to bear witness to the truth. Everyone who is of the truth hears My voice" (Jn 18:37).

As Pilate listened to this King of Truth, he felt rising within the impulse for higher things. But the thought of an unworldly King was too much for him; and as the first Pragmatist of Christian times, turning his back, he sneered the question of the twentieth century: "What is truth?" (Jn 18:38). And with those momentous words the worldly rejected the un-worldly, which is God. And so Christ became the only King in the whole history of the world who ever stumbled to His throne. The world was certain that no King could be a success who was such a failure. But such are the ways of God. Many times, during His public life, He said that those who loved Him would be hated by the world; that He would draw men to Himself by being lifted up on a cross in seeming defeat; that the greatest love man can show is to lay down his life for his sheep. Now the solemn hour had struck. The King was hanging on a peg. For a crown He wore a wreath of thorns; for a scepter, an iron nail; for a throne a cross; for royal purple, His own Blood; for His army, those who shouted: "If he is the King of Israel, let him come down now from the cross" (Mt 27:42); for his courtroom, the Hill of the Skull; for his courtiers, thieves; and for his battle-cry: "Father, forgive them, for they know not what they do" (Lk 23:34).

When the King was enthroned, those who expected a worldly king and not an unworldly God who loves to the folly of dying, saw an inscription above the cross painted on wood in huge red letters. It was written in three languages of which at least one was known by every single man in that multi-tude — in the official Latin, the current Greek, and the vernacular Hebrew — informing all that this

Man whom the world rejected and who loves when hated — this Man dying between two common thieves in the sight of the world was: "The King of the Jews."

The mob rushed back to Pilate swearing they would not have Christ rule over them, and they said to him: "Don't write, 'The King of the Jews' but 'He said, I am the King of the Jews'" (Jn 19:21). Pilate's courage, which had oozed away so rapidly at the name of Caesar, now revived, and the Procurator cut them short with the last words ever recorded of him — "What I have written, I have written" (Jn 19:22). Pilate had written, and it would stand. The royalty of Christ must be promulgated in the Hebrew which is the language of the People of God, in Greek which is the language of the doctors of philosophy, and in Latin which is the language of the world. It was not the King who was unworthy of His kingdom, but the kingdom that was unworthy of the King.

When evening came, and the scene was darkened, and the cry of thirst rang out over the hills, splitting the rocks and opening graves, its echo rang down the corridors of time until it comes knocking at the portals of our own heart in this very day and this very hour. It comes to the men of our day who have tried to be human without God, and who found that if they lived without God, they were not men, but beasts; it comes to the disillusioned bodies who made a religion out of flesh and reminds them

that the soul as well as the body must have its joys
— its "passionless passion and wild tranquillities":
Jesu voluptas cordium. It comes to those whose religion is science, and makes them shift uneasily as
they try to explain law without a Lawmaker and
order without Mind — which is God.

But it is one thing to recognize the insuffi-
ciency of the world, and quite another thing to
acknowledge that the King of hearts and wills and
nations is One who brings a cross and the dull hard
lesson of mortification. Face to face with One whose
Kingdom is within, the entrance to which can be
gained only by carrying a cross like the King with the
Cross, there is a dreadful fear lest having Him we can
have nothing else. Can it be, we say to ourselves, that
His love is like a bitter weed which suffers "no flower
except its own to mount"? Can we be courtiers in the
service of a King who wears purple robes and is
cypress crowned? Must all His harvest fields of love
"be dunged with rotten death"? Must the charcoal of
our lives pass through fire before He can trace His
portrait on our soul? Must the sun spend itself to
light a world, and the glory of the cloud die in
passing showers before there can spring forth fruit
or flowers? Must the seed die before it can bud forth
life, and must the Cross be the condition of the
crown; and the three hours' crucifixion with the
King be the prelude to an eternal glory with Him in
Heaven?

As we turn these questions over in our minds, there comes to us the Voice of the King like the bursting sea:

> Lo! all things fly thee, for thou fliest Me!
>   Strange, piteous, futile thing!
> Wherefore should any set thee love apart?
> Seeing none but I makes much of naught
>   (He said),
> "And human love needs human meriting:
>   How hast thou merited —
> Of all man's clotted clay the dingiest clot?
>   Alack, thou knowest not
> How little worthy of any love thou art!
> Whom wilt thou find to love ignoble thee,
>   Save Me, save only Me?"[6]

The human heart now begins to see the light. He is not just a King who failed — He is a King who failed in the eyes of the world to win eternal victory in the eyes of God. Hence if we are to reign with Him in Heaven, we must begin our reign with Him on earth, as He began His, namely, on a Cross. It is the unworldly thing to do — yes. The world first feasts, and then has its fast; it gluts itself and then loathes its excesses; it laughs and then weeps. But the King of the Cross reverses the order: the poor shall not always be poor; the crucified shall not be always on

---

[6] *Ibid.*

a cross; the poor shall be rich; the lowly shall be exalted; those who sow in tears shall reap in joy; those who mourn shall be comforted; and those who suffer with Christ shall reign with Him. The solution is clear: What we call pain, sorrow, and crucifixion, is "but the shade of His Hand outstretched caressingly." At last the soul is conquered by the Beauty of the King so lately known, so lately loved, as that Divine King whispers gently the secret of His seemingly hard way with us:

> All which I took from thee I did but take,
>   Not for thy harms,
> But just that thou might'st seek it in My arms.
>   All which thy child's mistake
> Fancies as lost, I have stored for thee at home:
>   Rise, clasp My hand, and come![7]

---

[7] *Ibid.*

GOD'S BRIDGE-BUILDER

VIII

GOD'S BRIDGE-BUILDER

I F THE MODERN MIND WERE asked what thing in the world it would like most to discover, it would probably answer: the missing link. Every now and then we hear of its discovery — but it is only a rumor. The most annoying feature of the missing link is that it is missing.

There is nothing wrong in seeking the missing link, but it does seem to be a rather absurd emphasis on the wrong thing. Why should we be so concerned about the link which binds us to the beast, and so little concerned about the link which binds us to God? Why should the deep secrets of man's being be sought in the slime of the earth, rather than in the rarefied atmosphere of the Kingdom of Heaven? Even though the link were found, it would only tell us the source of that lower part of our nature, which we have in common with beasts; but it would tell us nothing about the higher part which we have in common with God. A thing is to be judged not by that which is lowest in its makeup, but by that which is highest and noblest. So it is a far more profitable quest not to seek the link imprisoned in the dust which binds us to an animal, but rather the link suspended from Heaven, which binds us unto God.

A link or bond there must be between God and man. Man is sinful, God is holy; and there is nothing common between the two. Man is finite, God is infinite; and there is nothing common between the two. Man is human, God is Divine; and there is nothing common between the two. By my own power I am not able to touch the ceiling of my room, but the link of a ladder would effect a union between the two. In like manner, if there were ever to be a real communion between Heaven and earth, between God and man, there would have to be a link between the two. Those who seek the missing link between the man and the animal say that that link must have something common to both. In like manner, we, who seek the link between God and man, say that that link must be both human and Divine.

Where seek that link? In a cave? Yes! The world is right in seeking the Cave Man, but it is seeking him in the wrong cave. If we are to find the prototype of man we must seek it not in the cave of Moulin, but in the cave of Bethlehem, and the name of that Cave Man is not Pithecanthropus but Christ; the light shining in his eyes is not the light of a beast coming to the dawn of reason, but the light of a God coming to the darkness of men; the animals in the cave are not wild beasts shrieking at one who came *from* them, but the ox and the ass bowing down to one who came *to* them; the companions in the cave are not wild creatures with lifted clubs as a sign of war, but Joseph and Mary with folded hands as a symbol of peace. In a word, *Christ is the link* between the finite and the infinite, between God and man, because finite in His human nature, infinite in His Divine, and one in the unity of His Person; missing, because men have lost Him; Pontiff, because the Bridge-Builder between earth and Heaven, for such is the meaning of Pontiff; Mediator, because the High Ambassador of God amongst men. All these names are only other ways of saying that which we forget was the life of Christ above all things else — the life of a Priest.

What is a Priest? A Priest is an intermediary or link between God and man. His mission is to do two things: to bring God to man by the infusion of Divine Life; and to bring man to God by redeeming man from sin. This Our Lord declared was the double purpose of His coming into this world: "I've come that you might have life, and have it more abundantly" (Jn 10:10); and, "The Son of man came, not to be served, but to serve, and to give His life as a ransom for many" (Mt 20:28).

The first purpose of the Priesthood of Christ is to bring God to man or Divine Life to human life. We have no right to say there is no higher life than ours, any more than the worm has a right to say there is no higher life than its life. The very fact that man is never satisfied with his mere earthly life is a proof of something beyond. Like a giant, imprisoned bird, his wings beat uneasily against the gilded cage of space and time. He has always sought to be more than he is: that is why he has ideals; that is why he has hopes; that is why the Roman emperors called themselves gods; that is why man, when he forgets the true God adores himself as god. But man can never acquire that higher life by his own power, any more than he can change a stone into a serpent. If he is to be possessed of a higher life, it must be given to him from above. If the animal is to live the higher life of man, it must surrender its lower existence and be reborn in man, who comes down to it to take it up as food. If man is to live the higher life of God, he must die to his lower life of the flesh and be reborn to the higher life of the Spirit who comes down to him with that Divine Life. This is the message Our Lord gave the carnal-minded Nicodemus who, hearing it, said: "How can a man be born when he is old? Surely he can't go into his mother's womb and be born a second time?" (Jn 3:4). The Savior replied that He meant not a fleshly birth, but that spiritual regeneration of water through which man was reborn as a child of God.

And yet how few there are who want to live it! The sweet complaint of the Savior at the beginning of His public life is true of our own day: "And you don't want to come to Me that you may have life... I've come in my Father's name, yet you don't receive Me" (Jn 5:40, 43). The result is that while the body of the modern man is fed, his soul is left to starve. Starve it will until the great inspiration of life ceases to be economics, or the science of earthly goods and begins to be theology or the science of the life of God.

The second function of the priestly life of Christ consisted not only in linking the life of God to man, but also in reconciling man to God by redeeming him from sin. Many of the emasculated lives of Christ today picture Him merely as a moral reformer, a teacher of humanitarian ethics, or a sentimental lover of birds and beasts. Our Lord is primarily none of these things. He is first and foremost a Redeemer. In that He breaks with all reformers and preachers who ever lived. Take any of them: Buddha, Plato, Confucius, Socrates, Lao-tsze — why did they come into the world? Each and every one of them came into this world to live. But why did Our Lord come into this world? *He came into the world to die.* It was the supreme business which engaged Him from the day of His birth: "The Son of man," He said of Himself, "came to seek out and save what was lost" (Lk 19:10).

Socrates, on the contrary, came into the world to teach. Hence the greatest tragedy of his life was the cup of hemlock juice which interrupted his teaching. Death was his greatest stumbling block, the one supreme obstacle and annoyance which spoiled his conversations about truth. But the Cross was not to Christ what the hemlock juice was to Socrates. It was not the interruption of His life — it was the very beginning. His teaching was not stopped by His death. It was His death that proved His teaching true.

Buddha came into the world to preach the philosophy of renunciation. He was a philosopher and only a philosopher. His supreme business in life was solely and uniquely to explain defeat — in a certain sense fatalism. Death spoiled his preachments about renunciation. But death to Christ was not what death was to Buddha. Both preached renunciation. Death was the end of Buddha's preaching about renunciation. Death to Christ *was* the renunciation. Death was the end for Buddha. But for Christ it was only the beginning.

Our Lord did not walk about the earth forever telling people platitudes about truth. He was not just explaining truth, defeat, resignation, sacrifice. Every one else did this. The goal He was seeking was death. From the beginning to the end, only one vision was before His eyes — *He was going to die*. Not die because He could not help it, but die because He willed it. Death was not an incident in His career; it was not an accident in His plan — it was the one business He had to do. All during His redeeming life

He looked forward to His redemptive death. He anticipated His blood-shedding on Calvary by His circumcision at eight days of age. At the beginning of His public ministry His presence inspired John to cry out to his disciples at the Jordan: "Here is the Lamb of God" (Jn 1:36). He answered to the confession of His Divinity by Peter at Caesarea-Philippi that He "would have to suffer greatly and be rejected by the elders and the chief priests and scribes, and be put to death and rise after three days" (Mk 8:31); the leaden-weighted days caused Him to cry out in beautiful impatience: "I have a baptism to be baptized with, and how apprehensive I am until it is accomplished!" (Lk 12:50). To the member of the Sanhedrin who would seek a sign, He foretold His death on the Cross. He answered: "And just as Moses lifted up the serpent in the desert, so must the Son of Man be lifted up so that everyone who believes in Him will not die but will have eternal life" (Jn 3:16). To the Pharisees, who were as sheep without a shepherd, He spoke: "I am the *good* shepherd. The good shepherd lays down his life for his sheep... And I lay down My life for My sheep... No one takes it from Me; on the contrary, I lay it down on My own. I have power to lay it down and I have power to take it up again. This is the command I've received from My Father" (Jn 10:11, 15, 18). To all men of all times who would forget that He came as Our Redeemer and Savior, He speaks the most tender words that were ever caught up on this sinful earth: "For God so loved the world that He gave His only begotten Son, so that everyone who believes in Him will not die but will have eternal life. For God didn't send His Son into the world to judge the world, but to save the world through Him" (Jn 3:16-17).

But why did Death play such an important role in the Divine plan? How did Death bring man to God? Death brought man to God by blotting out the debt of sin. Man was a sinner. He could no more restore himself to the favor of God than a man who owes a million dollars can pay it with a cent, or a soldier who is mortally wounded can bind up his own wounds. Our Lord willed to pay the debt of man by suffering for man, for death voluntarily undergone is the supreme proof of love. "Greater love than this no man has — to lay down his life for his friends" (Jn 15:13). How could satisfaction be made, save by One whose intrinsic worth might tender some worthy offering from a boundless love to a perfect justice? How was a real reconciliation between God and man possible, unless the Reconciler had the capacity for mediating, unless He could represent God to man no less truly than man to God. In other words He had to be a priest — a link between God and man because true God and true man. Being man He could freely suffer and freely die but being God His suffering would have an infinite value. Sacrifice from the beginning of time has been through the shedding of blood, for sin in a certain sense is in the blood. Our Lord therefore, as man, resolved to pour it out, even to the last drop, to express at one and the same time God's hatred of sin and God's love of man. Only the righteous can adequately pay for injustice; only the perfect can discount the crimes of the brute; only the rich can cancel the debts of great debtors; only a God in His Infinite Goodness can expiate the sins which man has committed against Him. Only Christ can redeem. But when He takes the Cross, the wants of the body are forgotten in the wants of love.

Why the darkened heavens? Why the rent veil in the Temple? Why the shattered rocks? Why do the dead come from their graves and walk the city of the living? Why did the sun hide its face? If Nature could have been given a tongue she would have answered that her Lord was crucified. But her convulsive homage before the Cross of Christ is as nothing when compared to a moral miracle of which the only sensible symptoms are a promise of pardon to a repentant sinner at His right. Not when Christ raised the dead, not when He rebuked the seas and the winds, not when He shone in His glory on Tabor, but when He was crucified, pierced with nails, insulted, spit upon, reproached, and reviled, did He show His power to change the heart of a thief, draw to Himself a soul that once was harder than the rocks, and in an embrace of love promise: "Amen, I say to you, this day you'll be with Me in Paradise" (Lk 23:43). That promise was the revelation of the depth and height of His Redemptive Power — a flash of the Eternal Lightning of the Godhead, illumining the true meaning of His humiliation as man.

He who is upright like a Priest and prostrate as a Victim is Our Lord and Savior Jesus Christ. The day the Holy Spirit poured out the ointment of Divinity on His human nature in the sanctuary of the Virgin Womb was the day of His ordination; His teaching in Galilee and Judaea was His seminary — for what is a seminary but a place where seed is sown; the surrender of His Will in constant obedience to the Will of His Father was the offertory; the mount of Calvary where He performed the last and solemn act of His priesthood was the Cathedral; the cross suspended between Heaven and earth, in reconciliation of both, was His altar; the crimson that poured out from the precious wardrobe of His side was the royal vestment of sacrifice; the sun turning to red at the horrors it saw was the sanctuary lamp; the Body which He gave as Bread was the host; the blood which He poured out like water was the priceless wine; the separation of both by the crucifixion and the act of His will was the consecration; and His last words commending His soul to the hands of the heavenly Father was the *Ite Missa est*.

Would that our civilization would cease turning over the dust of the primeval jungles in search of the link that ties us to the beast, and begin to kneel before the uplifted cross on the rocks of Calvary in search of the link that binds us to God; would that the world ceased regarding Our Lord only as a teacher and began to adore Him as a Priest, who brings God to man by the gift of Divine Life, and man to God by the gift of Divine pardon; would that men stopped building their bridges across the chasm of time to bind themselves to earth and began building their bridges across the abyss of eternity to bind themselves to God. Then the crucifix would once more come unto its own. Then some broken heart would kneel before the crucifix even for a minute to learn the sweetest of all sweet messages — that regardless of how sinful he is, he must be worth something, since the God-Man died on a cross for love of him.

DIVINE INTIMACIES

IX

DIVINE INTIMACIES

AT TIMES SOME PEOPLE FEEL that Divine Love is very far away while the love of creatures is very close and real. Yet this is not the truth; it is the love of God which is burning, and the unsteady devotion of the love of creatures which is cold and bitter. To prove this we need only go into the sanctuary of our own heart; and distil out of it the intimacies of love, and we will see how God has satisfied them far beyond the wildest dreams and most ardent hopes. In other words, God reveals His love in terms of the intimacies of the human heart.

What, then, are the different degrees or intimacies of love? The first intimacy of love is speech. We would never know anyone loved us, unless that person told us so. Speech might be called the summation of a soul; all that it has been, all that it is, and all that it will ever be — we need only to hear a person speak and we can say: "he is a proud man"; "he is a humble man"; "he is a cruel man"; "he is a charitable man." Even the written words of those who lived and spoke centuries ago reveal their characters, their passions, their failings and their ideals. One need but open the books of the ancient past and there we see the heart of a Socrates, the heart of a Caesar, the heart of a Cicero revealed in every word that dropped from their lips. Speech, then, is the first form of the intimacies of love.

Now if God reveals Himself to us in terms of the human heart, then He should show His love for us by speaking to us. And God has spoken! The speech of God is Revelation. Open Sacred Scripture at any page and you will find written down the voice of God speaking to us His message of love: — "With an everlasting love I have loved you; so I have kept My mercy toward you" (Jr 31:3); "Though your sins be like scarlet, they may become white as snow; though they be crimson red, they may become white as wool" (Is 1:18).

So on throughout the pages of the revealed word of God. But is that all love can do? Is there not yet another intimacy of love beyond speech? Does not the human heart crave for other communications besides the sense of hearing? Does it not also want to see the one who speaks the words of love? Does it not want to see words born on human lips, see the earnestness of a visage, the flash of an eye, the sincerity of a heart written on the openness of a face? Not long can love be satisfied with words behind a veil, or words in a book. As intimacy grows, love also demands vision. Love wants to be present with the one loved; that is why Love naturally tends towards an Incarnation. Hence if God is to exhaust all the intimacies of love, and speak to us in the language of the human heart, He must not only be heard, He must also be seen! And God was seen! That was the Incarnation of Our Lord and Savior Jesus Christ. He who dwelt in inaccessible light was seen by shepherds and Wise Men under the light of a star. He who made the universe and its myriad of dancing suns and whirling planets was seen fixing the flat roofs of Nazarene homes; He who lived in the inexhaustible riches of the Kingdom of Heaven was seen as a poor village tradesman in the little town of Nazareth; He who is the very Word of Wisdom of the Godhead was seen in the companionship of fishermen whose knowledge rose no higher than the low country of Galilean lakes. Men heard God say that He was love. Now they saw Love in action. Men had heard God say He would forgive sins; now they saw Him confer that power on His Apostles unto the end of time. He was so often seen in attitudes of love and pardon that it is embarrassing to choose among them. One of the most touching certainly is the day He pardoned the woman taken in sin (Jn 8:3-11). The scribes and Pharisees were surrounding a woman who was prostrate on the ground, with a veil drawn about her to hide her from the accusing fingers. She was an adulteress; the scribes and Pharisees were her self-righteous judges. Each of them held a stone in his hand prepared to cast it at the poor defenseless creature. Occasionally one of them would reach to the hand of his neighbor, take from it his stone, weigh both, and then return the lighter stone, that he might cast the heavier one upon the woman. Just as they were about to execute judgment, they saw Our Blessed Lord approaching and resolved to catch Him and ensnare Him in His speech. Either He had to condemn the woman, or He had to release the woman. If He released the woman He would be disobeying the law of Moses, which was the law of God, according to which any woman guilty of adultery was to be taken outside the city gates and stoned. If He condemned the woman, He would not be merciful, and He said that He was merciful. In either case, they thought, He was trapped.

But the dilemma of justice or pardon was no great dilemma to Him who solved it in the Incarnation. Our Lord detested adultery; but He also detested the hounding of merciless hypocrites. He stooped over and with His fingers wrote in the sands — the only time in His life He ever wrote. What did He write? He probably wrote on the sands of that hillside the sins of the woman, and as He wrote the winds blew them away. Then He probably drew back a few paces and wrote again as He saw the sins of the Pharisees — but this time where the winds would not blow them away. As He wrote, He spoke:

"Let whoever is without sin among you be the first to throw a stone at her" (Jn 8:7). Upon hearing this the scribes and Pharisees began to leave, but according to legend not all at once. Some few remained. Our Lord looked up at one of them with one of those deep, calm, penetrating looks, then stooped over again and wrote in the sands; and ancient tradition says He wrote the word "Thief"; whereupon the accuser dropped his stone and fled. Then He looked at another and wrote in the sands the word "Murderer"; and he likewise dropped his stone and fled. Finally, looking at the sole survivor with a look that pierced his heart and anticipated the terrible judgment, He leaned over and wrote in the sands the word "Adulterer"; and he too dropped his stone and fled. None of the actors in the scene remained but two — the criminal and the Judge — the contrast of sin and Divinity.

No longer was any voice crying for her blood; no longer was any hand uplifted for her death. There was now no one with her but Innocence; the only One who had a right to throw a stone, but who threw none. Lifting His eyes from the sands He said to her: "Woman, where are they? Has no one condemned you?"

And she answered: "No one, Lord."

"Neither do I condemn you. Go your way, and from now on sin no more" (Jn 8:10-11).

Strange verdict it was that Day passed on

night, that Virtue passed on vice! At last men saw the Love of God at work, saying to penitent sinners of that day and of our own: "You are black, but I send you the sun; you are unworthy to live, but you shall live to be worthy; I despise your sin, but I love you, the sinner. I condemn you; I forgive you; I blame your rotten past; I wipe it out forever. Go now and sin no more." Oh! she might have wished to have murmured a word of thanks, but as she looked upon the Love of God visible to men, she saw Him with His head lowered, the silky waves of His hair shining in the sun, as His finger traced in the sands the outline of a bleeding heart.

Love wishes to hear the speech of the one loved; love also wishes to see the one loved; but is that all that love can do? Does there not yet remain even one other intimacy by which love can betray and reveal itself to the human heart? There still remains one other intimacy of love, an intimacy so profound, so delicate, so personal, so complete that the greatest insult anyone can offer us who knows us not, is to make use of it — and that is the intimacy of touch. Anyone may hear the one loved; anyone may see the one loved; but only the intimates may touch the one loved.

If God is to exhaust all the intimacies of love, then He must not only speak to us, He must not only be seen by us, but He must also touch and be touched. And He was touched! The children were touched by the hands that made them; the woman suffering from an issue of blood touched the hem of the garments of God. Thomas too touched Him as he put fingers in hand, and hand in heart to be cured of his doubt. But one of the sweetest of all the touches was that which He received in the home of Simon the Pharisee.

Simon was that type of man who was fond of lionizing strangers. Not because he was a devout follower of Our Lord, but because of the great fame of the Galilean teacher, he invited Our Lord to his rich table. Some little ceremonies, such as the host kissing his guest and anointing his hair, were omitted from the occasion. Simon probably felt that since Our Lord was only a rustic Rabbi, not too familiar with the best society, there could be some deficits in etiquette.

The guests reclined at table according to a custom recently introduced into Palestine from the East — each leaning on his left elbow, leaving the right hand free to eat at table. As the bronzed servants were bringing in the precious viands, an untoward incident happened. Simon looked up to the far corner of the room, and what he saw brought a blush to his cheek. He would not have minded it, if anyone else had been there — but the Rabbi! What would He think of it? He was just about to order the intruder removed, but a look from the Master deterred him.

The intruder was a woman. Her name was Mary; her city, Magdala; her profession, a sinner. She moved slowly through the silk purple curtain which hung about her. As her luxuriant hair fell across her eyes, she did not attempt to brush it away, for it acted as a screen against the gaze of the Pharisee. The room had now grown quite still. Suddenly a sad, little sound broke the quiet. It was a sob. The woman was weeping. Standing now over the feet of the Divine Savior, she let fall upon the sandaled harbingers of peace a few tears, like the first warm drops of a summer rain. She tried to wipe them away with her hair, but the fountain flowed on, as if answering to the deepest misery of life.

Then she remembered she had concealed under her veil a vessel of precious ointment pressed from the best of God's creation. But what did she do with it? She did not do what you and I would have done. What would we do? We would take the vessel of precious ointment, pour it out, slowly — deliberately... resolutely... drop... by... drop... as if to indicate by the very slowness of our giving the generosity of our gift. Not so with Magdalene! Not so with those who really love! She broke the vessel and gave everything, for love knows no limits. She saw nothing and felt nothing except an inexpressible delight, in which joy is pain and sorrow is joy, in which tears, the common fount of joy and sorrow, unite in one mighty ecstatic emotion.

All the while Simon was thinking the vile thoughts of that endless cemetery of whitened sepulchers who are outside clean and inside full of dead men's bones. So he muttered to himself: "If this fellow were a prophet he'd realize who and what kind of woman this is who's touching him — that she's a sinner" (Lk 7:39).

And Our Lord reading his thoughts said to him: "Simon, I have something to say to you."

"Speak, Teacher."

"Two men were debtors of a certain money-lender; the one owed five hundred *denarii*, the other, fifty. When they were unable to repay, he forgave them both. Which of them, then, will love him more?"

"I suppose the one to whom he forgave the most."

"You've judged correctly," He said… "Her sins, many as they are, have been forgiven, because she has shown great love" (Lk 7:40-47).

"Because she has shown great love."

Mary seemed to have heard those words between sighs. But she could not believe her ears. Did He really speak to her — she who summed up within herself forty centuries of sin; she the type of woman who gave away her body without giving her soul; she who seasoned her jests with sins; she whom women envied and detested; whom men desired and defamed. Could it be that He was kind?

She looked up at Him for some assurance that she had heard aright. His eyes became illumined like two altar fires; His lips, fine and keen with feeling, began to move. Then came the silence that always precedes the speech of God: "Your sins are forgiven... Go in peace!" (Lk 7:48, 50).

The Shepherd was happy — He had found the lost sheep. The lost sheep was happy, for in sounding the depths of love, she had touched the very feet of God.

There is nothing more that Love can do; there is no other tongue by which the heart may speak. Love has three and only three intimacies: speech, vision, and touch. These three intimacies God has chosen to make His love intelligible to our poor hearts. God has spoken; He told us that He loves us: that is Revelation. God has been seen: that is the Incarnation. God has touched us by His grace: that is Redemption. Well indeed, therefore, may He say: "What more could I do for My vineyard than I have done? What other proof could I give of My love than to exhaust Myself in the intimacies of love? What else could I do to show that My own Sacred Heart is not less generous than your own?"

If we answer these questions aright, then we will begin to repay love with love. Then we will not ask, "How much must I do?" but "How much *can* I do for love of Him?" Then we will return speech with speech which will be our prayer; vision with vision which will be our faith; touch with touch, which will be our communion. Then one day when we think the chalice of our poor hearts has been emptied of the last drop of love for Him, He shall take us to Heaven where our hearts shall be filled to overflowing with the fountain of joy and where there shall be no speech but the song of angels, no vision but the Lamb of God, and no touch but the embrace of the "passionless passion" and "wild tranquillity" of the Everlasting Love — which is God!

THE DEPTHS OF SIMPLICITY

X

THE DEPTHS OF SIMPLICITY

T HE WORLD HAS ONE SUPREME test for character, and that is the possession of a virtue in a high and eminent degree. Many generals, for example, in our national history are ranked as men of great character because of their valor, and many scientists are ranked as men of great character because of their wisdom. Some are judged noble because of their love of peace, others because of their bravery in war; some because of their majesty, and others because of their gentleness; some because of their wisdom, others because of their simplicity.

But this is not the real way to judge character. The possession of one virtue in an eminent degree no more makes a great man than one wing makes a bird. Just as the eagle's power is measured by the distance from the extremity of one wing to the extremity of the other, so a man's character is to be judged, not by the possession of one extreme virtue but by the expanse between that virtue and the opposite one which complements it. Christian character is nothing more nor less than the reconciling of opposite virtues. In other words, a really great character is not just a brave man, for if a man were brave without being tender, he might very easily become cruel. Tenderness is what might be called the other wing to bravery. In like manner, majesty alone does not make character, for majesty without gentleness might very soon degenerate into pride. Love of peace alone does not make character, for without the opposite virtue of courage, peacefulness could very easily slip into a spineless cowardice. Wisdom without simplicity makes a man proud; simplicity without wisdom makes a man a simpleton. A person of real character therefore does not possess a virtue on a given point on the circumference without, at the same time, possessing the complementary virtue which is diametrically opposed to it; for what is character, but the tension between opposites, the equilibrium between extremes. Thus St. Paul exhibits in his life the beautiful tension between zeal and gentleness; St. John the tension between overflowing love and uncompromising devotion to truth; and Moses the tension between firmness and meekness.

Just as every engine must have its fly-wheel, every springtime its harvest, every ocean its ebb and its tide, so every person of really great character must have his or her pendulum so delicately adjusted that it can swing between the extremes of the magnanimous and the humble, the lofty and the plain, without ever once being detached. Character, then, is the balanced tension between opposite virtues.

It is in this sense that the character of Our Blessed Lord rises above all men and makes Him the Perfect Exemplar of goodness and the Paragon of virtues. One might show how He combined Majesty and Gentleness, Peacefulness and Force, Magnanimity and Humility, but for the sake of brevity we limit ourselves only to the two extreme virtues which He recommended to His Apostles at the beginning of His public life: Wisdom and Simplicity: "Be as wise as serpents and as guileless as doves" (Mt 10:16).

Our Blessed Lord did not make this recommendation without possessing it in an eminent degree Himself. He was wise with the Wisdom of God; but He was simple with the simplicity of a child. That is why He came to us as the world's God-Child. But what is more remarkable still, He never used His wisdom before the simple, but only before those who thought themselves wise. He was wisdom before the so-called wise, but He was simplicity before the simple. He exceeded the worldly wise with His wisdom and the simple with His simplicity.

First, He outdid the worldly wise with His wisdom. Take for example, the scene in the Temple at the beginning of His public ministry. The Passover was drawing near and pilgrims from Galilee began to gather into Jerusalem. Our Lord came with the throng and entered through the Golden Gate into the Temple. As He passed beneath the arch and came into the Court of the Gentiles, the open space before the steps that led up to the Holy Place, a busy scene lay before Him. It was more than the mere jostling of crowds paying their yearly tribute of half a shekel to the Temple Treasury. Rather here was a bedlam of confusion. In the heat of that April day were hundreds of merchants and shopkeepers mingling the cry of their wares with the bleating of sheep and the bellowing of oxen. There were little men with big wicker cages filled with doves, and under the very shadow of the arcades, sat the moneychangers wrangling in the most dishonest of trades, their greedy eyes aflame with the lust of gain. Everywhere there was huckstering, quarreling, bargaining, and the clanking of money to be heard above the chants of the Levites and the prayers of the Priests. And all this at the entrance to the Temple of the Most High.

When Our Blessed Lord entered, a righteous indignation laid hold of Him, for what is character but a beautiful tension between force and meekness. An anger divorced from meekness is but unsanctified passion, and meekness which cannot kindle into indignation is closely allied to moral collapse. And on the occasion, Our Lord's swift indignation was just as much a part of His Perfect Sanctity as His silent meekness in the hour of the Passion. He could not, being Justice itself, be silent before an offense against God. His eyes burned with a controlled anger; His firm face set in commanding scorn. His hands reached to some bits of binding cord lying on the floor beside Him. With His fingers, rapidly yet calmly, He knotted them into a whip. The traffickers stood still; the merchants eyed Him with growing fear; then they stepped back from Him as One Whom they had reason to fear.

Then quietly but firmly He began to move His tiny whip of knotted cord. The frightened crowd yielded, and sheep and cattle broke and fled. With His foot He overthrew the tables of the moneychangers, as they rushed to the floor to gather up their jangling coins from the filth and pollution. Before those who sold doves He stood still, for the dove was the offering of the poor, and there was less desecration in their lovely emblems of innocence and purity. To these He was more gentle. He did not scatter them; He did not break the baskets and release the doves; to their owners He spoke tenderly: "Get these out of here, and stop making my Father's house a place of trade" (cf. Mt 21:12-13 and Mk 11:15-19).

And His disciples seeing this transport of inspiring and glorious anger, recalled to mind what David had written of Him in prophecy: "Zeal for your house consumes me" (Ps 69:10).

And if we ask why the greedy traffickers did

not resist as their oxen were chased into the street and their money flung on the floor, the answer is because sin is weakness; because there is nothing in the world so utterly abject and helpless as a guilty conscience; because nothing is so invincible as the sweeping tide of Godlike indignation against all that is base or wrong; because vice cannot stand for a moment before Virtue's uplifted arm. Base and low as they were, every one of them who had a remnant of his soul not yet eaten away by infidelity and avarice knew that the Son of Man was right.

All the while there was standing on the marble steps that led up to the Holy of Holies, a group of Levites, scribes, and Pharisees who knew what a heavy loss that stampede would cause the merchants and themselves. They looked for the cause of the commotion and saw that He Who provoked it all was a carpenter from lowly Nazareth, with no mark of office about Him, no scrolls, no ensigns of dignity, but only an uplifted hand. They were indignant. How dare this obscure workingman with a few ill-smelling fishermen as companions arrogate authority to Himself within the Temple precincts, in which they alone were masters? They moved down the steps to Him, as He stood alone with the whip cord in His hand and asked Him: "By what authority do You do these things? Who gave You this authority?" (Mt 21:23 and Mk 11:28).

He might have pointed His finger at the panic-stricken crowd as a sign that all men fear the Justice of God. But these were learned men, skilled in the Scriptures, and wise in their own conceits. And before those who thought themselves wise, Our Blessed Lord was wiser. He would show to them a Wisdom, so deep, so profound, so revealing the truth of their Scripture, that not even they, the wise men of Israel, would understand. In fact, what He said was so deep that it took them almost three years to understand it. Firmly and solemnly with a gesture centered on Himself, He said something beyond their comprehension, something which in its apparent meaning filled them with perfect stupor and angry amazement because they understood not its depth. The words were over their heads, at the same time they stole into their hearts: "Destroy this Temple, and in three days I will raise it up" (Jn 2:19).

Destroy this Temple! This Temple, they thought, on which Solomon had lavished his wealth! This Temple on which ten thousand workmen enrolled as they brought the cedars of Lebanon to its walls! This Temple with its fragrant woods, embroidered veils, precious stones, glittering roofs! This Temple which was forty six years in the building and was far from finished! And this obscure Galilean youth bade them destroy it, and He would rebuild it in three days! Such was the false construction they put upon His words, because they were not wise enough to understand the wisdom of God.

Our Blessed Lord did not mean that earthly Temple before them, but the Temple of His Body. But why call His Body a Temple? Because a Temple is the place where God dwells. He was therefore equivalently saying: The real Temple in which God dwells is not that place of stone but this tabernacle of living flesh which I have taken from My mother, for I am the Holy of Holies: I am the Son of the Living God. I am the real Temple of the Most High!

Such Wisdom was too profound even for the wise of this earth. It was not until almost three years later that it began to dawn upon them, when the Temple they destroyed on Good Friday was rebuilt by the Power of God on Easter Sunday; and even the Truth, too, is so deep and profound that some of our wise men today have not yet begun to understand it even after nineteen hundred years.

Our Blessed Lord told His Apostles not only to be as wise as serpents, but also as simple as doves. And what He told them, He lived. He was not only wise with the Wisdom of God — He was simple with the simplicity of a child. This might be proved by His fondness for children whom His disciples one day forbade to come near Him. These Jesus reproved with, "Let the little children come to Me, and do not stop them, for of such as these is the Kingdom of God!" (Mk 10:14). And when He had folded them in His arms, laid His hands upon them and blessed them, He added once more the warning that we must have simple faith like little children, and that their ignorance is more illumined than the doctrines of wise men for only a clear and untarnished mirror can reflect the image of His Revelation.

But His simplicity is better indicated in His attitude to those grownup children of whom He said: "I praise You, Father, Lord of Heaven and earth, because You hid these things from the wise and intelligent and revealed them to mere babes" (Mt 11:25). A case very much in point is the simplicity of Our Lord before the Syro-Phoenician woman. In the middle of His public life, Our Blessed Lord, driven from Galilee, driven from Judaea, made His way as a wanderer on the earth to the coast of Syria where stood the cities of Tyre and Sidon fast falling into ruins. No sooner had He came into these cities, than a poor, infirm woman approached Him. She was a Gentile, and therefore what a Jew proud of his noble ancestry would call a contemptible Canaanite, what a Roman, whose subject she was, would call a Syro-Phoenician or a more or less degenerate Greek. She had a daughter, now growing up, who was suffering from an unclean spirit and quite mad. This shame obliged her to live rather apart from her neighbors.

But when she heard the great Wonder-Worker had come into her city, she felt she had to go and see Him, even though He was a Jew and she a Gentile. She ran to Him, and at a distance noticed He was kindly, gentle, and above all, simple. She heard her Jewish friends call him Lord: and others, "Son of David." She would call Him both and throwing herself at His feet with a piercing petition she cried: "Have mercy on me, Lord, Son of David! My daughter is severely tormented by a demon!" (Mt 15:22).

Our Lord did not look displeased but He answered her not a word, He walked on, testing her faith and her perseverance. But she walked on too, pleading, begging, and praying. The disciples bade her leave, but she refused. Becoming indignant at her annoying plea, they besought Our Lord, saying, "Send her away — she keeps crying out behind us" (Mt 15:23). Our Lord looked down at her sweetly, but what He said seemed to approve His disciples. "I was sent only to the lost sheep of the house of Israel," He told her. She seemed to sense it was not a rebuke, otherwise He would have sent her away as His disciples had bidden Him to do. He had not said He would not cure her daughter. He had only said His mission was first to His own people. She would try again — so she threw herself at His sacred feet in adoration and with more appeal than ever, looked into His eyes saying: "Lord, help me!" (Mt 15:25).

Could He remain untouched by that sorrow? Would He leave her to a lifelong agony of watching the paroxysms of her demoniac child? Calmly there came from those lips that never yet left unanswered a suppliant's prayer, words which reminded her that she was not of the house of Israel: "It isn't right to take the children's bread and throw it to the pups."

But not all the snows of Lebanon could quench the fires of love and hope which burned on the great altar of her heart, and prompt as an echo came, not an answer, but a glorious retort: "Yes, Lord — even the pups eat the crumbs that fall from their master's table" (Mt 15:27). If a self-wise Pharisee had made a retort of that kind, Our Lord would have withered Him with His wisdom, but when a simple soul makes a retort against Divinity and says she is only a puppy begging for a crumb, then He becomes so simple as to be seemingly vanquished by her simplicity. He Who exalted Himself amidst the proud humbles Himself before the humble; He Who was wise with His profound meaning of the word "Temple" before those who thought themselves wise, is now simple before a Syro-Phoenician with her simple turn of the word "pup." His heart expands, His lips move: "O woman, great is your faith! Let it be done for you as you wish" (Mt 15:28).

Wonderful wisdom! Wonderful simplicity! Such is the character of Christ. A God and a Child. Oh, will our world ever learn to imitate that beautiful tension between opposites? Will it go on dividing itself into the two classes of the educated and the uneducated, the literate and the illiterate, heaping praise on the so-called wise who reject the Wisdom of God and pouring scorn on the simple who accept it? Or will it someday, under the magic touch of Christ, discover that the truest wisdom is in being simple and the truest simplicity is in being Wise with the Wisdom of God. It is easy to be one or the other, but it is difficult to be both; just as it is easy to have nothing, and easy to possess everything, but it is difficult to live having nothing and yet possessing everything. That is why it is easy to be anything but a good Christian. It is hard to grow wiser and yet still be simple enough to want to be taught, and yet that is the condition of entering Heaven. No "old" people enter it — using old in the sense of those full of the conceits of years. Neither do the intelligentsia nor the sophisticated. "Whoever doesn't accept the Kingdom of God like a little child shall not enter it!" (Mk 10:15). There are only nurseries there!

GAMBLERS ON CALVARY

XI

GAMBLERS ON CALVARY

THE MOST TRAGIC WORDS ever written of Our Lord are those which John sets down in the beginning of his Gospel: "He came to His own… yet His own did not receive Him" (Jn 1:11). Bethlehem had no room for Him when He was born; Nazareth no room for Him while He lived; Jerusalem no room for Him when He died.

What happened then is happening today. The curtain never goes down on the great abiding drama of Calvary. In every century the same leading role is played by the Eternal Galilean. But new characters play the other roles. The story is always the same — the age-old story of indifference struck on a new key, in new hearts, and in new times. He still brings salvation, but men are indifferent to being saved. He still brings healing grace, but men are indifferent to their ills. He still comes to His own, but His own receive Him not.

Note the parallel between the indifference of some on Calvary and the indifference of some in our day. Recall that day when the Hosannas hushed, when palms withered and turned into spears, and the summer friends of victory made their flight with the winter of seeming defeat. Four judges, bands of soldiers, and a mad rabble in turn heaped opprobrium upon Him, and yet by the strangest of all strange miracles He grew in Majesty with each new insult. The more men treat Him vilely, the more beautiful He becomes; the more they abuse Him as a slave, the more He appears as a King. His very silence before Caiaphas and Herod was the silence of majesty. What right had they to judge Him Who was judge of the living and the dead! It was only when one of them appealed to the living God whence He came, that He makes the startling declaration that He is Divine. Even Pilate clothed in all the golden robes of Caesar's empire felt himself naked as he gazed upon the regal bearing of Him Who was clothed in the bright light of Divinity. No moral miracle in all the life of Christ surpasses in power the fact that in the hour of His humiliation He could influence a man as sordid as Pilate. In the life of no other man did Beauty and Majesty shine forth in the hour of greatest ignominy and scorn. Only a vague parallel to it is to be found in the Jewish people of old, whose loudest claims to spiritual primacy were uttered amidst the clanking of their chains, and whose superiority over all people was manifested as they sat enslaved amidst the false gods of Egypt.

At last the moment had come when the King took possession of the only Kingdom He would ever have upon this earth — the royal Kingdom of the Cross. Crowned not with the gold of the Magi, but with thorns of a yet impenitent nature, He begins the royal procession to an empire which was no wider than a beam of wood, but from which to a dying thief He could promise a Kingdom which was His even before the foundations of the earth were laid.

To the Roman executioners it was just another Roman holiday. Under a festal sky they led the procession to the Hill of the Skull where tradition marked the grave of Adam, and where the New Adam would now lay down His Life to take it up again. When their job was finished, and the last nail driven into His Throne a word of forgiveness bore into their hearts, they rested and divided the garments — for the Man on the cross had no further use for them. This was the perquisite of the executioners, and it came to them by law. Four soldiers divided the spoils, leaving only the tunic or seamless robe. It would be a sin to cut it, for after that it would be of no use to anyone; but one of them, an old gambler, took out his dice, threw them, and the tunic woven by His sinless Mother was awarded by luck to sinful men. Then in those terrible, simple words of the Gospel: "They sat down and kept watch over Him there" (Mt 27:36).

And what did they think of the Man Whom

they sat and watched? As the shadow of the cross fell about their dice they joked, gossiped, and gambled the hours away; they engrossed themselves in their own favorite topics of conversation, in mutual banter, and trifling little games. Now and then they glanced up with a curious interest. Once they looked up at Him as He promised pardon to a thief — but it was only a passing glance. Once again they gazed at Mary and wondered how any one could have such a beautiful Mother, and then how the Crucified could be even more beautiful than His Mother — but it was only a passing glance. They watched, but their minds were fixed on other things, on worldly pleasure, on reward, on money, on wine, on travel, on everything but the Mystery of the Cross.

But back to their games they went as "they sat and watched." They talked about the latest cock-fight in Jerusalem, about a wrestling match one of them had seen in Antioch; about the great chariot race that was to be run in Rome the coming Ides of May; about the gambling gains of a soldier of their garrison; about the possibility of Rome someday stamping Jerusalem under her heels; about the new dancing girl in the court of Herod; about the thousand and one indifferent things such individuals would talk about — everything, in a word, except about the one thing that mattered. And yet there, within a stone's throw of them — why, they might even have thrown their dice at Him! — was being enacted the tremendous drama of the Redemption of mankind; and *they only sat and watched*. Here they were in the presence of the most stupendous fact in the history of the world, actors in the supreme event for which all creation groaned, and they saw nothing.

And the three hours slipped by — opportunities soon pass. The young and Divine Body which suffered so much because it had so great a Soul, was now turned into a funeral pyre of suffering where all the suffering of the world burned together. As the executioners watched passively, He commends His Soul to His Heavenly Father, His friend at the right, to Paradise, His Mother to John; and *they only sat and watched*.

The scene changes — but the lesson remains ever the same. Divinity is still in the world, and the world receives it not. In all walks of life, the world goes on, gambling away the pearls of eternity for the tinsel of time, without ever once casting a glance at the Divinity Christ has left in His Church. If you would know where that Divinity is, then look for the Church that is ignored by men as Christ was ignored on Calvary. If you would find Divinity in the twentieth century, then look for that Church which they reject with the same crucifying indifference with which they rejected in the first century the Lord of Heaven and earth. Note the indifference in the field of education, international politics, and religion.

Go into the world of education, enter into the

university classroom and everywhere you will hear such wild ideas as these: the universe is due to chance; man is a mere accident in the evolution of the cosmos; the soul is a survival-belief of the Middle Ages; the new scientific spirit has antiquated the old morality; Christianity is a potpourri of pagan religions; truth purely ambulatory: we make it as we go; Christianity is founded on a false basis and therefore a man can have as many wives as he likes; religion is a remnant of primitive taboos; hell is a heritage of an age of fear and superstition, and God is a mental illusion which any psychologist can explain away.

This is the type of talk which is just as much pure nonsense as the gamblers on Calvary spoke — not a single idea of which will outlive the professors who teach them. And as these so-called learned men while away the precious moments given to discover the Truth which is God, while they seek the laws of the universe without ever once finding the Lawmaker, there stands in the midst of them — why, they even have thrown their books at it, as the soldiers might have thrown their dice — an institution which has been educating for two thousand years preserving for our age the best culture, art and philosophy of the past, leading to a definite knowledge of the end and purpose of being a man, and *they only sit and watch*. The suggestion that Truth may be in the Church is as absurd to them as the suggestion that Truth is pilloried to a Cross, and they only sit and watch.

Enter now into the broad field of international politics. Year after year, in Washington, London, Geneva, and Lausanne, the representatives of the great nations gather together in a really earnest desire to bind all people together in the bond of unity and peace. But year after year their treaties fail — and why? Because they have nothing outside the nations themselves to bind them. A man cannot wrap up a package if he is part of the package; a man cannot pack his valise if he is one of the articles that goes into the valise. In like manner nations cannot tie themselves into a league if they are parts of the league. And if they are parts of the league their treaties merely mean obeying some one else's politicians, and if we will not obey our own politicians, then heaven knows we will not obey some one else's politicians. There is only one thing in the world which can tie together all the nations of the world in the bond of peace, and that is something outside the nations themselves. But there is only one thing in the world which is not only international but also supra-national and that is the Church Whose Vicar is the spiritual father of all Christendom, and whose only force is the moral force of the Justice and Righteousness of Christ. As James Brown Scott, the secretary of the Carnegie Endowment for International Peace, has said:

> A dispute laid before the State of the Vatican for decision would be free from the suggestion of material force to compel its acceptance; would

be disconnected from any idea of territorial aggrandizement; would have a presumption of Justice in its behalf, because the State itself is a recognition of justice; and the decision, whatever it may be, is bound to be in conformity with the moral code of the centuries, and be dominated by a spiritual conception of things which temporal judges may sometimes be without.

And yet what is the attitude of nations in the face of this moral force which is above the nations because it is concerned with the salvation of souls? Year after year, the nations meet on the Calvary of the world's battlefields, throw the dice of international politics, discuss gold standards, long-range guns, and trade balances, and all the while there stands in the midst of them, someone who came to bring peace on earth and who might be the arbiter of nations because the spiritual force outside the nations — and *they only sit and watch.*

To suggest to our international politicians that the Vatican State is the only true moral Court of International Justice, would be just as absurd as to have suggested to the gamblers on Calvary that the Man on the Cross is the Moral Force of the World — but the Truth still remains: Salvation for nations resides in that which men so ignore, that in the presence of it they play their games of intrigue as *they only sit and watch.*

Finally, enter into the field of modern religion,

and witness the same indifference to the supreme truth of religion, namely that man is a fallen creature in need of the saving grace of Divine Redemption. There is no talk today of the saving of the soul, about the need of penance, about the Kingdom of God, about the Bread of Life; but there are countless emphases on the need of being broadminded; reiterated slogans about life being broader than logic, about one religion being just as good as another, about it making no difference what a man believes so long as he does not cheat or steal, about benevolence being the greatest virtue and excess of zeal being the greatest vice. Why, many a modern religious leader would regard you as a scoundrel if you told him he was not a gentleman, but would only smile on you benignantly if you told him he was not a Christian.

And all the while modern religion is feeding souls on husks, there stands in the midst of the religious world a Church which would satisfy man's desires for forgiveness by absolution, man's craving for union with God by communion, and man's yearning for truth with infallibility — and yet they only sit and watch. If they were told that Truth is one and that one opinion is not just as good as another, they would consider it just as absurd as the gamblers on Calvary would have considered the suggestion that Supreme Truth was hanging only on one of the Crosses. And as the Church proclaims to the world that God is Truth and Truth is One, they answer back: Can you not see that there are three Crosses on Calvary? How dare you assert that there is only one Truth? And so until the end of time the Church, as Christ, must go on being rejected, while the modern gamblers of Calvary, without making a distinction between Truth and thieves, between Eternal Life and the dying, *only sit and watch.*

And so, as Calvary is prolonged through time and space, we find that men are as indifferent to Divinity now as they were the day it was born in a crib and suffered on a Cross. Oh! for a love of Truth for which the hearts of men would burn! Oh, for the eradication of that spineless indifference which makes men play the games of earth on the altar steps of Redemption. Too long have we sat and watched with the gamblers and idlers of Calvary. It is now time to stand and adore and to revive the spirit of the days when men believed in Truth. I know the old age had its defects; I know it had its spirit of persecution, of narrowness, but these were only the excesses of *real* virtues — such as love of Truth. Instead of purifying them, we have taken them away root and branch and all, and now are indifferent to right and wrong, to good and evil. Anything is better than such torpor of a materialized people to whom God and eternity are as if they never existed. Anything is better than the fear of the responsibilities of Truth, which allow a restlessness, an ennui, a loathing and a doubt to creep into a soul, until it grows into a boredom.

Truth is all important. *Error is serious.* Hence before darkness settles over our lives let us see, that since Christ will not come down, we will have to get up, lest perchance while we play our games and throw our dice, we may miss the real lesson of the great Drama of Truth. There is only one gamble that is true and that is the gamble of Christ who took His life in the palm of His Hands, rolled it out in the blood-red drops of Redemption, and before the sun had set He knew that He had won. We can be gamblers like Him, for we can take the dice of this world, with its tinsel, its rusting treasures, its passing joys, and throw them for the everlasting crown of glory with Christ the King, and in that Hour of our Crucifixion, when we have thrown away all our lower self, and we think we have lost all, it shall prove to be, like the Savior's — the hour of our Greatest Victory.

THE CROSSES
OF LOVE AND HATE

XII

The Crosses of Love and Hate

I T IS MY GOOD FORTUNE TO BELONG to a Church which is hated. Truly indeed it is loved by those who know its Divine character; but it is also hated by thousands who regard it as antiquated, as behind the times, as superstitious, and even diabolic. It is spoken of as a Mother by those who receive its spiritual benefits, but it is so despised by others that it has been driven from some countries, has been tolerated by others, and regardless of how much other sects may differ among themselves, it is still considered their one common enemy.

A parallel of the attitude of the world to the Catholic Church is to be found in its attitude toward Christ. He too was loved; but He also was hated. We do not find such love toward any other person as we do toward Him; neither to we find such abiding hate. There is therefore a parallel between the two questions: why is Buddhism not hated, and why is Catholicism hated? and the two other questions: why is Buddha not hated, why is Christ hated?

First, a word about the love and hatred toward the person of Christ, and then about His Church. There are two great passions which entwine themselves around the life of Our Lord, as they do about no other person who ever lived: the passion of love and the passion of hate. He said He would be loved; He said He would be hated. He said He would be adored; He said He would be scorned. He said He would be loved unto folly; He said He would be hated unto fury and that the duel would go on until the end of time. Hate would lift Him up on a cross, but once on it He would lift all lovers unto His Heart which is love. "When I'm lifted up from the earth I shall draw all men to Myself" (Jn 12:32).

He said He would be loved more than fathers and mothers love children and more than children love fathers and mothers. This did not mean *not* loving parents, or *not* loving children. It meant only loving them *in Him*. He did not say we should love one another less, but only that we must love Him more. And is not this reasonable? Should not the whole be loved more than the part; should not the fire be preferred to the spark? Should not the circumference be loved more than the arc? The temple more than the pillar? Should not the Creator be loved more than His creatures? God be loved more than men, and Love loved more than the lovely?

Open the pages of history and name one single man who has ever been so loved after his death to a point of sacrifice and prayer. His cross has been deluged with tears of love in every age and century. To it all generations, as enthusiasts of love, have come crying out in the language of Paul: "Who will separate us from Christ's love? ... I'm convinced that neither death nor life, neither angels nor principalities, neither things present nor to come, nor powers, neither height nor depth nor any other created being will be able to separate us from God's love in Christ Jesus Our Lord" (Rm 8:35, 38-39).

Napoleon saw this as all great men saw it before him. In his isolation at St. Helena, he reflected upon the vanity of his own life and that of Louis XIV, of whom he said, "That great king is long dead, and even now he is alone in his room at Versailles, abandoned by the courtesans and perhaps the object of their scorn. He is no longer their master, he is a cadaver, a coffin, and a horror. Not long now and it shall be my lot too. That is what will happen to me. What an abyss between my profound misery and the reign of Jesus Christ, preached, loved, adored, and living in all the universe."

If you would prove it further, go lay your hand over certain hearts that receive Him in daily communion, and you will feel the flame that His Love has kindled. Go knock at the portals of the Carmelites, the Poor Clares, and the hundred other retreats of the saintly, and ask the question the world always foolishly asks such saintly souls, "Did you enter into this place of prayer because you were disappointed in love?" And the answer that will flash back to you will be, "No, I am not here because I was disappointed in love. I was never disappointed in love. My first love is my only love — the Eternal Love of my Lord and my God."

There is no need of multiplying witnesses. Even your very thirst for perfect love is a thirst for Him for Whom you were made, and without Whom you cannot be happy. He sought love in poor, weak, frail hearts like our own, and unlike any other heart that ever beat, His Sacred Heart has been loved above all things else, even life. There is only one conclusion we can draw, in the language of Pascal: "Jesus Christ wished to be loved. He is loved, therefore He is God."

Now, let us turn to the other fact about the life of Our Lord which proves He is Divine; and that is hate. Hated He said He would be — by the world until the end of time — not the material universe, not by people in general in it, but hated rather by what His own Apostles have called the spirit of the world.

Recall some of the incidents of His Life, and you will see how the world hated Him from the very beginning. When only eight days of age the venerable old Simeon told His Mother that He was a sign to be contradicted, which was just a paraphrase of John's tragic note, that He came into the world and the world received Him not. When still under two years of age the soldiers of Herod drew swords to slaughter the Innocents in a vain attempt to kill Innocence. Then later on in the full bloom and blossom of life, picture this Humble Artisan with His Apostles on the very night before He died, looking down the corridors of time and saying to all future generations that He would be hated by the world. That hatred would be so personal, He went on to say, that any one who loved Him would in turn be hated by the world. "If the world hates you, remember that it hated Me before you. If you had been of the world, the world would have loved its own, but because you're not of the world, but instead I chose you from the world, therefore the world hates you. Remember the word I spoke to you, 'A servant is not greater than his lord.' If they persecuted Me, they'll also persecute you... But they'll do all these things to you because of My name, because they don't know the One Who sent Me" (Jn 15:20-21).

He shall be hated! What a peculiar prophecy! What had He ever done to be hated? He was meek and humble of heart. His life He offered for the redemption of many. His Gospel was the Gospel of love, even for his enemies. His last act was pardon and forgiveness for those who put Him to death. It was all a hatred, as He said, "without cause." There was a terrible perversity about it all. He healed their wounds, and they wounded Him. He brought back their dead to life, and they took away His life. He called men from evil to good, and yet evil men nailed Him to a cross. He brought Divine Life to make all men friends, and enemies gave Him an ignominious death.

Neither was there any reason for hating Him in those who loved Him. They were to be poor as He was poor; they strove to be perfect as their Heavenly Father was perfect, and humble like Him Who washed their feet. Even when persecuted, they rejoiced; when cursed, they blessed, as if the insult of wicked men was the consecration of their own goodness, and the mud thrown at them by the impure a pledge of their own purity.

There is nothing to hate in such a life, nor in such a doctrine. We must look outside of Him and His Gospel, then, if we are to find the reason for the immortality of that hatred. Can it be that He was an impostor and that His religion is an imposture? But if He is an impostor then our love for Him is false, and the world's hatred for Him is true. But if the world's hatred is true, then it ought to renovate society and transform human hearts. If our love for Him has done so much to remake men, and our love is a vain dream, then what great things the world's hatred ought to do which overthrows such an idol. But name one thing that the world's hatred for Our Lord has done. Where are the good works of such hatred? What peoples have been drawn from vice and corruption? What souls have been consoled? What hearts have been sweetened? There are men and women in the world dying in sorrow, crying out for the bread of everlasting life, and there are sinful hearts pleading there for forgiveness. Where, oh! where — oh, Hatred of Christ — is your consolation, your mercy and your peace for such souls?

No, the hatred of Christ is not to be found in the fact that He was an impostor, for hatred is a negation, and the negation is an assertion of His existence. There are too many minds in all ages who have studied and bent the knee, to admit He was an impostor. Where then find a reason for the hatred?

There must be some reason peculiar to Him and Him alone which accounts for it. In no one else in all history do you find an abiding hatred except against Our Lord. No other founder of a world religion ever said He would be hated, and no one ever was hated. Buddha is not hated. Mohammed is not hated. Zoroaster is not hated. Some men while they lived were hated. Nero was hated while he lived, even by his own countrymen. Genghis Khan was hated by a great mass of humanity. Bismarck was hated by many of his own countrymen. But who hates any of them today? There are no fists uplifted in desecration against Nero. There are no oaths of bitterness against Genghis Khan. There is no hymn of hatred sung over the tomb of Bismarck. Hatred died with them. Not even the Kaiser, who was hated by part of the world and by some of his own people after the First World War, is hated today.

Now why has hatred died against every one else, and still endures against Our Blessed Lord? Here we come to the real reason. What causes hatred? Hatred is caused by that which annoys or creates an obstacle to something we desire. Why was Nero hated when alive? Because his vices were an obstacle to social justice for which the Romans yearned. But now that Nero's vices are corrupted with his flesh, no one hates him. No one today hates Tiberius, Domitian, Ivan the Terrible, or Nestorius. Even the word contempt is too strong for them. They have ceased to be objects of hatred, because they have ceased to be obstacles. But with Our Lord it is different. The hatred against Christ has never weakened even after twenty centuries; and the reason it still endures is because Christ is still an obstacle — an obstacle to sin, to selfishness, to godlessness, and to the spirit of the world. The Spirit of Christ still lives in those who love. He is still a hindrance to nations who would forget God; still a stumbling block to those who cease to pray; still a reproach to those who sin and atone not; still a Divinity refusing to step down from the cross to win the plaudits of an hour; still a Voice calling uneasy hearts away from the spirit of the world to the glorious liberty of the children of God. Hatred still endures, because He still lives. But if He still lives, then He is Divine. If He is Divine, then until the spirit of the world dies, there shall be distress for His followers. But when it dies, victory. "You'll have suffering in the world, but take courage! I have conquered the world" (Jn 16:33).

Here is the key to the hatred of the Church — Our Lord was intensely loved and intensely hated because He was Divine. Only the perversion of the sovereign love of God could ever explain such hate. Only that which continues that Divine Life could ever be the object of such a hate.

> If there is a form of Christianity now in the world [says Newman] which is accused of gross super-stition, of borrowing its rites and customs from the heathen and of ascribing to forms and cer-emonies an occult virtue; a religion which is considered to burden and enslave the mind by its requisitions, to address itself to the weak-minded and ignorant, to be supported by sophistry and imposture, and to contradict reason and exalt mere irrational faith; a religion which impresses on the serious mind very distressing views of the guilt and consequences of sin, sets upon the minute acts of the day, one by one, their definite value for praise or blame, and thus casts a grave shadow over the future; a religion which holds up to admiration the surrender of wealth, and disables serious persons from enjoying it if they would; a religion, the doctrines of which, be they good or bad, are to the generality of men un-

known; which is considered to bear on its very surface signs of folly and falsehood so distinct that a glance suffices to judge of it, and that careful examination is preposterous; a religion such that men look at a convert to it with curiosity, suspicion, fear, disgust, as the case may be, as if something strange had befallen him, as if he had had an initiation into a mystery, and had come into communion with dreadful influences, as if he were now one of a confederacy which claimed him, absorbed him, stripped him of his personality, reduced him to a mere organ or instruments of a whole; a religion which men hate as proselytizing, anti-social, revolutionary, as dividing families, separating chief friends, corrupting the maxims of government, making mock at law, dissolving the empire, the enemy of human nature, and a conspirator against its rights and privileges; — a religion which they consider the champion and instrument of darkness, and a pollution calling down upon the land the anger of heaven; a religion which they associate with intrigue and conspiracy, which they speak about in whispers, which they detect by anticipation in whatever goes wrong, and to which they impute whatever is accountable; a religion, the very name of which they cast out as evil, and use simply as a bad epithet, and which from the impulse of self-preservation they would persecute if they could; if there be such a religion now in the world, it is not unlike Christianity as that same world viewed it, when first it came forth from its Divine Author.

If you would find Christ today, then find the Church that does not get along with the world. Look for the Church that is hated by the world, as Christ was hated by the world. Look for the Church which is accused of being behind the times, as Our Lord was accused of being ignorant and never having learned. Look for the Church which men sneer at as socially inferior, as they sneered at Our Lord because He came from Nazareth. Look for the Church which is accused of having a devil, as Our Lord was accused of being possessed by Beelzebub, the Prince of Devils. Look for the Church which, in seasons of bigotry, men say must be destroyed in the name of God, as men crucified Christ and thought they had done a service to God. Look for the Church which the world rejects because it claims it is infallible, as Pilate rejected Christ because He called Himself the Truth. Look for the Church which is rejected by the world as Our Lord was rejected by men. Look for the Church which amid the confusion of conflicting opinions, its members love as they love Christ, and respect its Voice as the very voice of its Founder, and the suspicion will grow, that if the Church is unpopular with the spirit of the world, then it is unworldly, and if it is unworldly, it is otherworldly. Since it is otherworldly it is infinitely loved and infinitely hated as was Christ Himself. But only that which is Divine can be infinitely hated and infinitely loved. Therefore, the Church is Divine. Therefore it is the life of Christ among men! Therefore we love it! Therefore we hope to die in its Blessed Embrace!

THE CROSS AND THE CRUCIFIX

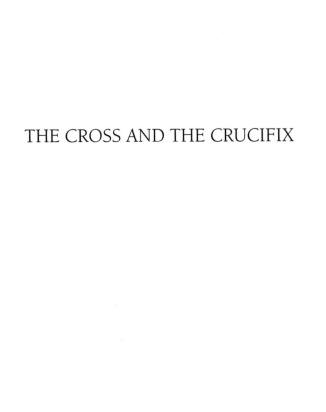

XIII

THE CROSS AND THE CRUCIFIX

The first question ever asked in the history of the world, and the one which brought us pain and woe, was the question, "Why?" It was Satan, the first skeptic, who asked the question, "Why did God command you not to eat from any of the trees in the Garden of Paradise?" (cf. Gn 3:1). From that time until this, our poor little minds have asked many "whys," but none more often than: "Why is there pain in the world?" "Why does suffering exist side by side with luxury?"

This problem of pain has a symbol, and the symbol is the cross. But why is the cross typical of the problem of suffering? Because it is made up of two bars, one horizontal and the other vertical. The horizontal bar is the bar of death, for death is prone, prostrate, flat. The vertical bar is the bar of life, for all life is erect, upright. The crossing of one bar with the other signifies the contradiction of life and death, joy and sorrow, laughter and tears, pleasure and pain, our will and God's will. The only way a cross can ever be made is by laying the bar of joy against the bar of sorrow; or, to put it another way, our will is the horizontal bar, God's will is the vertical bar; as soon as we place our desires and our wills against God's desires and God's will, we form a cross. Thus the cross is the symbol of pain and suffering.

If the cross is the symbol of the problem of pain, the Crucifix is its solution. The difference between the cross and the Crucifix is Christ. Once our Lord, Who is Love Itself, mounts the cross, He reveals how pain can be transformed through love into a joyful sacrifice, how those who sow in tears may reap in joy, how those who mourn may be comforted, how those who suffer with Him may reign with Him, and how those who take up a cross for a brief Good Friday will possess happiness for an eternal Easter Sunday. Love is, as it were, the joint where the horizontal bar of death and the vertical bar of life become reconciled in the doctrine that all life is through death.

Here is where the solution of Our Lord differs from every other solution of the problem of pain, even those solutions which mask themselves under the name of Christian. The world meets the problem of pain either by denying it, or by attempting to make it insoluble. It is denied by a peculiar process of self-hypnotism which would say that pain is imaginary and due to want of faith; it is made insoluble by an attempt to escape or flee it, for the modern man feels it is better to sin than to suffer. Our Lord, on the contrary, does not deny pain; He does not attempt to escape it. He faces it, and by doing so proves that suffering is not foreign even to a God become Man.

Pain has, therefore, a definite part to play in life. It is a remarkable fact that our sensibilities are more developed for pain than for pleasure, and our power for suffering is in excess of our power for joy. Pleasure increases to a point of satiety, and we feel that if it went beyond that point, it would become a positive torture. Pain, on the contrary, goes on increasing and increasing, even when we have cried "enough"; it reaches a point where we feel we can bear it no longer, and yet it unburdens itself until it kills. I believe the reason why we have greater capacity for pain than pleasure is because God intended that those who lead a sound moral life, should drink the last drop of the chalice of bitterness here below, for there is no bitterness in Heaven. But the morally good never quite sound the depths of pleasure here below, for greater happiness awaits them in Heaven. But whatever the real reason, the truth still remains that on the cross Our Lord shows that love can take no other form, when it is brought into contact with evil, than the form of pain. To overcome evil with good, one must suffer unjustly. The lesson of the Crucifix, then, is that pain is never to be isolated or separated from love. The Crucifix does not mean pain; it means sacrifice. In other words, it tells us, first, pain is sacrifice without love; and secondly, that sacrifice is pain with love.

First, pain is sacrifice without love. The Crucifixion is not a glorification of pain as pain. The Christian attitude of mortification has sometimes been misrepresented as idealizing pain, as if God were more pleased with us when we suffered, than when we rejoiced. *No!* Pain in itself has no sanctifying influence! The natural effect of pain is to individualize us, center our thoughts on ourselves, and make our infirmity the excuse for every comfort and attention. All the afflictions of the body, such as penance, mortification, have no tendency in themselves to make men better. They often make a man worse. When pain is divorced from love, it leads a man to wish others were as he is; it makes him cruel, hateful, bitter. When pain is unsanctified by affection, it scars, burns up all our finer sensibilities of the soul, and leaves the soul fierce and brutal. Pain as pain, then, is not an ideal: it is a curse, when separated from love, for rather than making one's soul better, it makes it worse by scorching it.

Now let us turn to the other side of the picture. Pain is not to be denied; it is not to be escaped. It is to be met with love and made a sacrifice. Analyze your own experience, and do not your heart and mind say that love is capable of overruling, in some way, your natural feelings about pain; that some things which otherwise might be painful are a joy to you when you find they benefit others. Love, in other words, can transmute pain and make it sacrifice, which is always a joy. If you lose a sum of money, is not your loss softened by the discovery that it was found by some very poor person whom you loved? If your head is racked with pain, your body wasted and worn from long vigils by the bedside of your child, is not the pain softened by the thought that through your love and devotion, the child was nursed back again to health? You could never have felt the joy, nor had the faintest idea of what your love was, if that sacrifice had been denied you. But if your love were absent, then the sacrifice would have been a pain, vexation, and annoyance.

The truth gradually emerges that our highest happiness consists in the feeling that another's good is purchased by our sacrifice; that the reason why pain is bitter is because we have no one to love and for whom we might suffer. Love is the only force in the world which can make pain bearable, and it makes it more than bearable by transforming it into the joy of sacrifice.

Now, if the dross of pain can be transmuted into the gold of sacrifice by the alchemy of love, then it follows the deeper our love, the less the sense of pain, and the keener our joy of sacrifice. But there is no love greater than the love of Him Who laid down

His life for His friends. Hence, the more intensely we love His holy purposes, the more zealous we are for His kingdom, the more devoted we are to the greater glory of Our Lord and Savior, the more we will rejoice in any sacrifice that will bring even a single soul to His Sacred Heart. Such is the explanation of a Paul who gloried in his infirmities and of the Apostles who rejoiced that they could suffer for Jesus Whom they loved. That, too, is why the only recorded time in the life of Our Lord that He ever sang was the night He went out to His death for the love and redemption of men.

No wonder saints have always said that the best and greatest gift which God could ever give them would be the privilege He gave His Son, namely, to be used and sacrificed for the best and greatest end. Nothing else could ever so much please them as to renew Christ's life in theirs; to complement His work in their own; to fill up in their bodies the sufferings which were wanting to the passion of their Lord. The world would take away pain. The Crucifix would transform it by love, by reminding us that pain is from sin and sacrifice from love, and nothing is nobler than sacrifice.

> The cry of earth's anguish went up unto
> God —
> Lord, take away pain, —
> The shadow that darkens the world Thou hast
> made,

The close coiling chain
That strangles the heart, the burden that
       weighs
On the wings that would soar, —
Lord, take away pain from the world Thou
       hast made
That it love Thee the more.

Then answered the Lord to the world He had
       made:
Shall I take away pain?
And with it the power of the soul to endure
Made strong by the strain?
Shall I take away pity that knits heart to heart
And sacrifice high?
Will ye lose all your heroes who lift from the
       flame
White brows to the sky?
Shall I take away love that redeems with a
       price
And smiles through the loss, —
Can ye spare from those lives that would
       climb unto Mine,
The Christ on His Cross?[1]

No, the world cannot spare the "Christ on His
Cross." That is the reason the world is sad. Having
forgotten Him, it is in pain. And oh! what a waste of
pain there is in the world! How many aching heads
there are which are never united with a Head crowned

---

[1] Anonymous.

with thorns for the Redemption of the world; how many lame feet there are whose pains are never softened by a love for those other Feet which climbed the great hill of Calvary; how many bruised bodies there are which, knowing not the love of Christ for them, have no love to soften their pains; how many aching hearts there are who are in pain because they have no great love, such as that of the Sacred Heart; how many souls there are who look at the cross instead of the Crucifix, who have the pain without the sacrifice, who never seem to learn that just as it is through want of love that pain arises, so it is later on through want of love that hell arises; how many souls there are who have missed the joy of sacrifice because they have never loved! Oh, how sweet is the sacrifice of those who suffer because they love the Love Who sacrificed Himself for them on a cross. To them alone comes an understanding of the holy purposes of God, for only those who walk in darkness ever see the stars.

THE SEVEN SORROWS OF MARY

XIV

THE SEVEN SORROWS OF MARY

The Prophecy of Simeon

FORTY DAYS HAD PASSED SINCE the angels sang their Glorias to the white chalked hills of Bethlehem. It was now the second day of February. According to Jewish Law, every mother after giving birth to a male child was to present herself at the Temple of Jerusalem to be purified, and to offer her child to God in testimony that all gifts come from Him. And thus it was that the Lord of the Temple was brought to the Temple of the Lord.

The proper offering on such occasions was a yearling lamb for a burnt offering and a young pigeon or turtle dove for a sin offering. The poor were permitted by the merciful Mosaic legislation to bring instead either two turtle doves or two pigeons. Such was the offering of Mary who possessed no wealth except the riches of the Lord of Heaven and earth.

The priest at the Temple on that day was

Simeon, a devout Israelite already bent with the burden of years, but happy in the Divine Intimation that he would not die until he had seen the Messiah Who was to come. Simeon was the living representative and symbol of the old Jewish Law which for forty centuries had been expecting the Redeemer; he was the end of the race of Adam, the crown of the Old Testament, the fruit of its maturity, the end and consummation of Israel's gift to the world.

When Our Blessed Mother laid the Divine Child in his arms, it was the moment of union of the Old and New Testaments, or better, the passage from the Old to the New. That gesture meant that all the promises of the Old Testament were accomplished and all the prophecies of God's chosen people fulfilled. Antiquity had said its last word. History, which had until now recorded its battles and set down the rise and fall of its kingdoms as events before Christ, would henceforth write them down as happening in the year of Our Lord.

Once Simeon's weary arms bore the weight of the Eternal and yet refused to break; once aged Simeon embraced Youth Who was before all ages; he could now take his leave, close the book of prophecies and bid adieu to his own life. And so in that age when old men cease to sing, Simeon opened the vents of song, and in the silence of the Temple, there arose like sweet-smelling incense, the sweet strains of the *Nunc Dimittis*. It was the compline of his life, as it is now the daily compline of the Church, the song the Church will sing in her old age when the Lord comes in the clouds of heaven on the day of the sunset of the world:

"Lord, now you let your servant go in peace; your word has been fulfilled: my own eyes have seen the salvation which you have prepared in the sight of every people: a light to reveal you to the nations and the glory of your people Israel" (Lk 2:29-32).

But all that light which flooded Mary's soul was soon obscured, as a black cloud sometimes hides from us the face of the sun. Simeon's words of joy turned into sorrow, as he spoke of the part Mother and Son were to play in the Redemption of the world:

"Behold [this child] is destined to bring about the fall and rise of many in Israel, and to be a sign that will be opposed. And a sword will pierce your own soul so that the thoughts of many hearts may be revealed" (Lk 2:32-35).

It was a solemn announcement that she was to guard the Victim until the Hour of Sacrifice and be the Shepherdess until the Lamb should be led to slaughter on the sign of contradiction, which is the cross. It was an echo back to the Garden of Eden, where a tree brought the ruin of the first Adam, and at whose gates stood an angel with a flaming sword to guard the gates until the appointed hour of salvation. Simeon was now saying that the hour had come. The tree of Paradise that brought ruin would be transplanted to Calvary and be His cross; the sword of the angel would be lifted from his hands and driven into Mary's heart, as a first witness that only those who are pierced through and through with the sword of sacrificial love shall enter the everlasting Eden of Heaven.

"A sign of contradiction!" "A sign that will be opposed!" Mary did not need to wait for Calvary's cross! She saw now that He Who is Love, would be hated; that He Who is Peace, would be a pretext for war; that He Who is Life, would be an occasion for death; that He Who is Truth, would be the theme of all errors and heresies until the end of time; that He Who is Light would drive souls away by the very splendor of His Light; that He Who came to save the world, would be contradicted and crucified by the world; that He would be the touchstone of all hearts; that from now on men would have to take sides; that there would be no more one-fisted battles, no more half-drawn swords, no more divided loyalties; that souls would either gather with Him, or they would scatter, and that their opposition to Mercy would make their rejection the more fatal and merciless.

As Mary left the Temple that day she understood as she never understood before why the Magi brought with their joyous gifts of gold and incense, the bitter, sad, and sorrowful gift of myrrh. She saw now that the law that bound Him would also bind her, and that while He would have the tree, she would have the sword; that as He was the new Adam, she would be the new Eve; and as Eve was instrumental in the fall, so she would be instrumental in the salvation as the Co-Redemptrix of the Redeemer Christ.

Prayer

Mary, if you had been disjoined from your Divine Son, like a quiet peaceful garden with the sun playing on it, far away from the storm-enveloped glory of Calvary, you would never have been really Our Mother. How terrible the sea of human sorrows would be were not your moonlight shining upon it! But now that you are called to co-redeem with Our Redeemer, you have become the Mother of all the afflicted! Wipe away our tears, for you understand our sorrow; mend our broken hearts, for yours was broken too. Draw out all swords, for the hilt is in your hand. Mary, you are the Mother of Sorrows; if you were not, then you could never be the Cause of Our Joy.

The Flight into Egypt

Centuries and centuries ago, the people of Israel in Egyptian bondage made their Exodus to the Promised Land. History now reverses itself. The Exodus is toward Egypt, and the leader is not Moses but the

Infant Savior. The occasion which prompted it was the order of Herod the Great, that all male children under two years of age in Bethlehem should be put to death by the sword. Herod heard from the Wise Men that they sought a Child Who was to be a King, and he was fearful of his power, as if He Who brought the golden Kingship of Heaven would ever think of taking away the tinsel kingship of earth. But the Wise Men did not return to Herod after seeing the Child — one always takes a different road back after seeing God. Herod's jealousy may have been aroused by the prophecy (later recorded by Tacitus) "that from Judea was to come the Master and Ruler of the world." Tacitus' fellow Roman historian Suetonius quoted a contemporary author to the effect that the Romans were so fearful about a King who would rule the world that they ordered all children born that year to be killed — an order that was not fulfilled, except by Herod.

Herod may have recalled these things, but in any case he ordered the massacre of the innocent children. His whole career was red with the blood of murder. He caused his brother-in-law, the young Aristobulus, to be drowned before his eyes; he ordered the strangulation of his favorite wife, the Princess Mariamne; his three sons, and the father and mother of his wife likewise perished by the sword; and even those who survived were more miserable than those who suffered. Hence it was not hard for him to order a slaughter of the Babes, for their blood was but a drop in the crimson river of crime. It was hard on the poor mothers of Bethlehem whose cries mingle with Rachel who would not be consoled, but it was harder still on Mary, whose only crime was that she bore in her arms a Child Who sheathed the beautiful grandeur of the Godhead in the scabbard of an infant's flesh.

On a dark night when poor mothers who denied her a home on Christmas eve wandered homeless through the streets, an angel appeared and bade Joseph take Mary and the Child and flee into Egypt. Mary had no treasures to gather up, but only the Treasure which she bore in her arms. The wilderness, the desert, heathendom confronted her. And as the night winds stirred, and the moon, which was one day to be pictured beneath her feet, now shone upon her head, she stole out of Bethlehem into the sands. Another Joseph was going with her and the Child into Egypt, to save it again from a famine, not with the meat which perishes but with the Bread which endures unto Life everlasting.

This exile of the Creator from His chosen creatures was the second sword to pierce the Heart of Mary. It was all the more keen, because her Child was hated!

Why should any one hate a Babe? What had He done to a king that he should be so unkingly? Jesus was hated! And yet He was more helpless than herself. She knew how lovable He was, and how much welcome He deserved after four thousand years of waiting. Why, then, should they make Him fly before He was able to walk?

The bitterness of this sorrow was that it seemed — I say only seemed — to be so much outside the order of Divine Providence. We all can easily bear the sorrows which come to us directly from God; His very fingers which reach tiny crosses to us seem to lighten them by His touch. The sorrows of the other mothers were softened in later years by the sweet thought that God did not permit their children to grow up and shout "Hosanna" on Sunday and "Crucify" on Friday. They saw that their sorrow was directly from God. A sickness we can bear, or even a death, because they too come directly from God. But the injustice and ingratitude of men! That is the more terrible, because we never know when it will end! God is more merciful. Thus when David, because of his sin of pride, was offered a choice of punishment, the injustice of men or a pestilence, he cried out: "Let us fall by the hand of God, for He is most merciful; but let me not fall by the hand of man" (2 S 24:14). And so he chose the pestilence.

Mary's sorrow was of that more bitter kind — it came from the wickedness of men! From the injustice of a pagan! It therefore seemed all the more terrible because God did not seem to have a hand in it. But added to it all was the tragedy that this sad note had to be struck far down in the scale of sorrows — in a stranger's land, away from home.

Prayer

Mary, by this your second sorrow teach us that God's ways are hidden in everything, even in those things that seem as far away as Egypt. Often during our life, when we are asked to leave the peace and quiet of religious contemplation where we are so much at home, to take up those duties and tasks of a work-a-day world, which seem in comparison, like an Egyptian exile, remind us that there is nothing in life that cannot be spiritualized and turned into a prayer, provided we do it in union with your Son! Mary, I am slow to learn, tardy to understand, reluctant to dare, but impress me with the great truth that we can make a Holy Land out of the pagan Egypt of our daily toil, provided we bring with us your Infant Child.

The Three Days' Loss

The only time artists ever represent Our Blessed Mother without her Child is when she is joyfully looking up to Heaven, as in the Immaculate Conception. But there was one time when she was childless and did not look up, and that was when she looked down to the desert in the sorrowful quest of her Child. Our Blessed Lord was then twelve years of age. It was the age at which, according to Jewish legend, Moses had left the house of Pharaoh's daughter; and Solomon had given the judgment which first revealed his wisdom, and Josiah had first dreamed of his great reform.

In that year, He went up to Jerusalem at the Passover with Mary and Joseph, and according to tradition He went on foot. Nazareth, their home, was about eighty miles distant from Jerusalem. Leaving the garland of hills which encircle the little town like the petals of an opening flower, they made their way to the Holy City where the profane plumage of the eagle wings of Rome was swinging from the gates, through which they passed into the Temple for the celebration of the Pasch. Many an old man in that Temple was sighing at the memory of better days when the great Isaiah and Jeremiah thrilled all Israel with their prophecies. And yet how feeble these great prophets were compared to a venerable man and beautiful mother kneeling on the Temple steps with a Child between them Whose Name was Eternal, and yet who was only a dozen years of age as we count circling seasons and emptying moons. Why, the choirs of angels must have hushed as the prayers of God the Son on earth, floated away into invisible shades to His Father Who is in Heaven! — Mary and Joseph must have ceased to look at the veil behind which stood the Holy of Holies, but fastened their gaze between them and confessed with ecstatic prayer the Divinity of the Boy Whose uplifted eyes were then fixed on the Heaven He left to set the world aright. The great mystery was that the very stones of the Temple did not cry out, and the sun stand still, and the cedars of Lebanon prostrate themselves in adoration of a God Whose earth-visiting feet were now bringing Eternity to Time. Was it not strange that earth should go on with its buying and its selling, its commerce and its wants, without so much as a smile of consciousness to the One Who was teaching us how to exchange humanity for Divinity and nothingness for everything!

When the Feast was over, the throngs departed, the men by one gate, the women by the other, to be reunited at the resting place for the night. The children went either with the father or the mother. Each suspecting the Divine Child was with the other, it was not until nightfall that His loss was discovered. Never before were there two such lonely hearts in all the world, not even when Adam and Eve were driven from the Garden of Pleasure. For three days they searched and finally found Him in the Temple expounding the Law to the Doctors and astounding them with His wisdom.

"When his parents saw Him they were amazed, and His mother said to Him: 'Son, why did You do this to us? You see Your father and I have been looking for You, worried to death!'

"And He said to them: 'Why were you looking

for Me? Didn't you know that I have to concern Myself with My Father's affairs?'" (Lk 2:48-49).

But Mary and Joseph must have searched for Him in the Temple the first day. Where was He then, and during the nights? We can only conjecture, but I love to think that He probably visited the future scenes of His Passion; stopped outside the Fortress of Antonia where Pilate would later try to wash His Blood from his hands; gazed in at the house of Annas who would later charge Him with blasphemy; made His way outside the city walls to a little hill where the world would erect a Cross and call it His Throne; and, finally, spent a night in the Garden of Gethsemane under the full Paschal moon where twenty-one years later His Apostles would sleep as He drank the bitter dregs from the Chalice of man's sin.

But wherever He was until the third day, in this third sorrow Mary's soul was plunged into the densest darkness, for she had lost her God! It was in this sorrow that the Mother Immaculate became in a more true sense the Refuge of Sinners. It strikes us first as a bit incongruous that she who was sinless should be the harbor of the sinful. How could she who never had remorse of conscience be a refuge for those whose conscience is full of bitterness? How could she who never lost her God know the pangs of a soul that through sin lost its God?

The answer is this. What is sin? Sin is separation from God. Now in these three days' loss Mary was physically separated from her Child, and she too had lost her God! The physical separation from her Child was but a symbol of the spiritual separation of men from God. The third dolor makes it possible for her to divine the feelings of sinners and still keep her soul inviolate. She knew what sin is. She too had lost her God! Thus she was suffering in atonement then for all minds who once had faith, and lost it; for all those souls who once loved God, and then forgot Him; for all those hearts who once prayed, and then abandoned Him. All the spiritual homesickness for Divinity, all the nostalgia for Heaven, and all the emptiness of hearts who emptied them of God, Mary felt as if it were her own — for now she was without the Redeemer. If an earthly mother weeps at the physical death of one of her children, what must have been Mary's grief at the spiritual death of millions of men whose Mother she was called to be by God!

Prayer

Mary, by this your third sorrow, teach us that if we should be so unfortunate as to lose God, we must not seek Him in new faiths, new cults and new fads, for He can be found only where we lost Him — in the Temple, in prayer, in His Church. Those other times when our soul is as arid as a desert, our hearts seem cold, and we find it hard to pray, and even begin to believe that perhaps God has forgotten us, because He seems to be so

*far away, whisper gently to us the sweet reminder
that, even when we seem to have lost Him, He is
still about His Father's business.*

Mary Meets Jesus Carrying the Cross

Twenty-one years have whirled away into space
since the third sorrow. During that time, eighteen
years were passed in the calm and quiet of a Nazarene
home. Mary's life was an endless ascension in love of
her role as the Co-Redemptrix of the world. Each
hour was like a novitiate in which she learned more
deeply her share of the Cross.

It is simply impossible to describe what it
means to spend eighteen years mothering God and
still being fathered by Him; eighteen years of receiv-
ing obedience from Him, and still being His sweet
slave of love! If God were not Love, we could never
use that word to describe the ecstatic life of Mary!

Jesus' very profession as a carpenter was a
reminder that one day He Who carpentered the
universe, was to be carpentered to a cross. Each
beam of wood He carried took Mary back to Isaac
carrying the wood of sacrifice to the hill of his death,
and forward to her Divine Son as the true Isaac who
would carry His own Cross to the Hill of Calvary.
Every nail in that carpenter shop suggested a cruci-

fixion, every thorn in their humble garden a crown, every tree a cross, and every red rose His crimsoned Self.

After those eighteen years she parted with Him. He was now thirty, and He must be about His Father's business. He had His thirty years of obeying; He would now have His three years of teaching, and then His three hours of Redeeming. The three years quickly passed, and He Who came to give testimony of the Truth saw Pilate, standing between the pillars of his judgment seat, wash his hands of Truth. He who said that no one would take away His Life, now prepares to lay it down. And on that terrible Good Friday morning Mary's solitary plea to Pilate was drowned in the raging storm of a thousand cries to "Crucify." The world had succeeded in contradicting Him, and in symbol of their triumph they gave Him the Cross. The procession began: There was the centurion leading; following were the heralds bearing the sign that would be nailed over the cross, the two thieves with their crosses, and the scribes and Pharisees who sent Him to death in the name of loyalty to Caesar — but the irony of that procession was, that it moved over a road scattered with withered palm branches. Mary followed, treading on the very Blood which she worshiped. She saw every drop of it; she saw the glittering spears, too, which looked like palms; she saw the thieves; she saw the weeping women; and yet she saw only one thing: Jesus bearing Eden's transplanted tree as she was wearing the angel's transported sword.

As if the approaching death had called forth the contrast, she thought of His sweet young days at Nazareth when she nursed Him, fed Him, knelt down with Him and even worshipped Him when He was asleep. Now she had Him no longer; everybody else had Him but her, and they were not adoring, but cursing. And yet for all that, she yearned for no thunderbolts from heaven to smite them, because she loved souls more. There is not a mother in all the world who would not rather receive pain from her son than have him bear it, but when that Son is God, then who shall measure the bitterness of her cup of Passion? In a certain sense her own Son was her executioner, because He was outdoing her in Love.

This new sorrow of Mary's was a revelation of her Son's words, that if we are to be His disciples we must take up our Cross and follow Him. Every life must climb to Calvary, not alone and unburdened with hands white and empty, but bearing the very instruments of crucifixion, the very elements of the sacrifice itself. As Isaac carried the wood of sacrifice, as Jesus carried His Cross, as the priest carries bread and wine to the altar, so Mary carries a cross in her own heart. The cross need not always be on one's shoulders: the sick in bed with burning fevers, the mother with her arms embracing children, the father at his daily toil, have no shoulders free for a cross, but they have a heart free for it, as Mary did. The spirit must go on even doing that which the flesh cannot do, for every act in the heart will be accounted equivalent to the work done. Simon for a moment relieved the shoulders of Jesus of His cross, but he did not relieve His Will to suffer. The crowd saw at that moment but one cross, and that was on the shoulders of the Cyrenian. There really were two, both hidden in the hearts of Mother and Son carrying their burden to the altar of Sacrifice.

Prayer

Mary, by this new sorrow, impress your poor children with the lesson of cross-bearing. Remind me that I may or may not give my love to Jesus, for I am master and captain of my soul, but that I am not free to accept His cross or to leave it. The choice is not between going through life with a cross, or going through life without it. I must take it. There is no way of walking around it — the outstretched arms will not permit me to do that. The choice is whether I shall accept it like you did, or have it thrust upon me, like Simon. Shall I be impelled to embrace it, or shall I be compelled to take it? Mary, let me see that the only real cross is the refusal to take it, and that by embracing it through love like you, it ceases to be a cross and becomes a scaffolding leading me on to the King-dom of God.

The Crucifixion

The Israelites during their wanderings in the desert were bitten by fiery serpents, whereupon Moses prayed that God might take them away. The Lord then said to Moses: "Make a saraph serpent and mount it on a pole, and if anyone who has been bitten looks at it, he will recover" (Nb 21:8). Centuries later when the Son of God came to earth He said to Nicodemus: "Just as Moses lifted up the serpent in the desert, so must the Son of Man be lifted up... so that everyone who believes in Him will not die but will have eternal life" (Jn 3:14, 16). Now the day comes when Christ, appearing in the form of sinful man, was to be lifted up on the Cross, that all who looked upon Him might be healed of the sting of sin.

As He mounted His throne when the cross swung into its pit, the earth shook in protest against killing the God Who trod its hills and walked its lakes; the sun went into eclipse at high noon in protest against the snuffing out of the Light of the World; the lambs for the Temple sacrifice protested too by bleating more mournfully than ever at the passing of their Shepherd, the Lamb of God. But there was no protest in His heart. We listen in vain for any expression of physical suffering. When His silence is broken, it is never to utter a complaint. His personal life was buried, as if all the wants of His Body were forgotten in the wants of love. It would seem as if the print of the nails had impressed upon Him not His own pains, but the pains of others. And what was true of Him, was true of His Mother also. She too seemed conscious that this was not a season of individual weeping, but a season of universal communion.

And as that great Chalice of all common miseries dripped silently, slowly, and mysteriously, the red drops of salvation, the hungry earth at its quaking opened its mouth to receive them, as if groaning more for redemption than the thirsty souls of men. The seven words rang from the Cross like seven swords into Mary's soul. It seemed that she was listening to Him sing His own funeral dirge. Any mother's heart would have broken at the sight of that Great Sanctuary Lamp of Life and Truth and Love emitting not red rays over Calvary, but dropping red beads in a rosary of redemption. Any mother would have collapsed at the vision of the beautiful wick of His Soul flickering in death as the wax of His Body and Blood burned itself away. Not all mothers' hearts have the same capacity for suffering; they vary with tenderness. The more delicate and tender the heart, the keener the suffering. But no mother in all the world has a heart as tender as the Mother of Motherhood. She was as delicate as a roseleaf, responsive to the gentlest breath of the evening breeze; hence her sorrow was so deep that even the greatest of martyrs have saluted her as their Queen.

It was all the more bitter because there was nothing she could do to ease her suffering Son. Grief must always be doing something, even if it is only stroking a fever-stricken brow, for the very wants of the one who suffers are the luxuries of the one who consoles. And yet what could Mary do? The pillow of the crown of thorns could not be smoothed; the bed of the Cross could not be freshened; the nails which folded in His hands and feet could not be taken away; even when He cried: "I thirst," there was nothing she could offer but her tears. Magdalene collapsed at His feet — it seemed she was always there in an attitude of penance. But Mary would not give way. The Evangelist who was at the Cross tells us that she *stood*. If Eve stood at the foot of the tree, she, the new Eve, would stand at the foot of the Cross — gazing upon a Crucifix.

And because she stood ready to serve, there came to her from the Cross her second Annunciation, not from the lips of an angel, but from the very mouth of God. Looking down from His Throne, Jesus saw her and John, His beloved disciple, and "He said to His Mother: Woman, here is your son. Then He said to the disciple: Here is your mother" (Jn 19:26-27). He called her not "Mother," but "Woman," to denote that she was now to become the universal mother of the human race which John symbolized. It was seemingly a poor exchange: a disciple for a Master; a creature for a Creator; a fisherman for a King; a son of Zebedee for the Son of God; and yet Mary accepted it gladly. She saw that just as at Bethlehem she became the Mother of God, she was now on Calvary to become the Mother of Men, and that just as at the Crib she begot the Captain of salvation, so now at the Cross she would bring forth His soldiers. She saw too that this could not be done without suffering, for although she brought forth the Innocent without pain, she could not bring forth sinners without sorrow. It would cost her her own Divine Son to become the Mother of Men but she would pay the price.

And thus her title as Mother of Men became hers not by mere external proclamation, but by the right of birth. Eve's curse hung upon her, that she would bring us forth in sorrow, and she accepted the penalty gladly. Thirty years with the Redeemer had taught her that she must love men as He loved them — enough to suffer and die for them, and still live on. She loved Him, because He was God; but she loved us, because it was God's will to save us. The first love was her martyrdom; the other her sacrifice. The one was like a tempest on the ocean, but the other was like its calm. Even in sorrow Peace was hers, for she was joined to an Eternal Father in the offering of a common Son.

Prayer

Mary, in your fourth sorrow you showed us how we are to carry our cross, and in this, the fifth you show us how to stand by it. Your Son has told us that only those who persevere until the end will be saved. But perseverance is sometimes so difficult. Few of us are, like you, willing to stand by the Cross for three full hours until the Crucifixion is ended. Most of us are deserters from Calvary, half-crucified souls; impatient to sit when we are not nailed to a cross. Many of us have high resolves in the dawn; but few sustain them through the day. Your own soul did not falter, because your Son's did not. He kept till evening the promise He had made to the morning sun rising red like blood. He had finished the work given Him to do. And you too stood by until the end of that sacrificial day. Beg for us the grace then, like you, to remain three full hours on Golgotha, so that when the lease on our life has ended, we can pray with Him and you: — "I have finished the work you gave me to do. Now, God, take me down, and lift me up into everlasting union with You."

The Taking Down From the Cross

And after three hours Christ died of thirst — not of a thirst for the pure water of Galilean brooks, nor the refreshing draughts of Jacob's well, nor the heart-warming wine of the Last Supper, but of a thirst for love, which came nearest to being quenched, not as a Roman reached Him vinegar and gall, but as an obscure thief reeling in the darkness of death gave Him the love of his bleeding heart. Christ was dead! The last cord of the Divine Harp snapped — it was the rupture of a heart through the rapture of love. He had died on the cross in the manner in which men willed, in the way in which He chose, and as His Heavenly Father consented. He had expiated up to the last. Now our expiation begins — but it is not yet finished.

Those who had not thought it a pollution to inaugurate their feast by the murder of their Messiah, were seriously alarmed lest the sanctity of the Sabbath, which began at sunset, should be profaned by three corpses hanging like red wrecks against a livid sky. Accordingly, soldiers came and broke the legs of the two thieves to hasten their death, and then coming to Jesus they found Him dead.

By not breaking His limbs they unwittingly fulfilled a prophecy over a thousand years old: that not a bone of His Body would be broken. One of the soldiers, Longinius by name, profaned the sanctuary by piercing the heart of Christ with a lance. The insult was Christ's, the pain was Mary's. Blood and water poured forth: Blood the price of our Redemption; water the symbol of our regeneration. Tradition tells us that when the first drops of that Liquid Love fell upon the infected eyes of Longinius, they were immediately cured. Mary rejoiced, because a greater miracle took place, as Longinius believed in the One Whose Heart he pierced.

There now came to the hill of sorrow two notable citizens of Jerusalem and the Sanhedrin: Joseph of Arimathea and Nicodemus — the twilight companions who before wanted to be friends of Christ and yet not appear as such. Death energized these tepid souls, and now they came to weave with busy hands the flowers and wreaths of death. They placed the ladder against the Cross and mounted it while Mary, John and Magdalene remained beneath. It seemed fitting to Mary that Joseph should be privileged to detach Jesus from His Cross, for it was her Joseph who, while living, was so often privileged to handle the limbs and touch the Flesh of the Incarnate Word. But he had gone to his rest, and now one that bore his name took his place. With gentle hands and adoring hearts the King Who staggered to His throne is now lifted from it in seeming defeat. Each nail is extracted from hands that even then might have lifted the portals of all the kingdoms of earth from their hinges. One wonders as the Nails, the Crown of Thorns, and the Cross came into Mary's hands if all Nature did not respond. The very iron in the dark womb of earth must have shuddered, because it had nailed its God. Every thorn must for the moment have hidden itself for shame under the petals of every red rose; every tree must have shaken in sorrow, because it bore the burden of the Crucified, and lifted its leafy arms in prayer that henceforth it would be cut by a sacrificial ax to become a cross beckoning hearts back again to God.

Finally the Body of the Savior was taken down and given to His Mother. It was like a red rose withering on her knee. The Prodigal Son was coming home again! A thousand memories surged through her aching heart. Through tear-dimmed eyes it seemed that Bethlehem had returned, for her Son was once more on her lap; Simeon seemed near her too as another sword of sorrow pierced her heart to the very hilt; one of the three kings seemed to visit her again as Nicodemus brought the myrrh for burial; even the anointing at Simeon's house was relived as Magdalene took up her post and anointed for burial the Feet which trod the everlasting hills.

Mothers live on last looks, and Mary must now take hers. As she looked, the sun setting in the golden tabernacle of the west threw on the hill the lengthening shadow of the Cross, as sorrow was now throwing its lengthening cross upon the heart of the Mother of the world. When she delivered her Son over for burial, she came as close to priesthood as any woman ever came, for was she not equivalently offering on the paten of her arms, the Immaculate Host of the Bread of Life. It was a great sorrow to give Him up, it seemed the world had Him so long, and she had Him so little but that was because she loved Him so much more. It was a poignant sorrow which would have been an inscrutable mystery to all mothers but her — but that was because her will was the will of God; to her sorrow is God's revelation; it is the wounded hand of Christ pushing aside the clouds which curtain His throne where all sorrow is turned to joy.

Prayer

Mary, most of us in moments of sorrow dispense ourselves from duties, refrain from work in the hour of our grieving, and look to human sympathy to ease our aching heart. But you, O sorrowful Mother, during this sixth sorrow, sought out no human consolation, in order to remind us that God loves most to come to lonely hearts which no other love can fill. Neither did you make your grief a burden to any one; you rather helped lay the Host on the Immaculate Corporal of your lap; your heart was broken, but no one knew it. By your calm resignation, dear Mother, teach us that our sorrow must never be in the way; that every cross we carry must be a cross only to ourselves; that Heaven most consoles the inconsolables of earth, and that a broken heart, like your own, is the favorite sanctuary of God.

The Burial of Jesus

One springtime Our Blessed Lord, gazing upon a laborer in his field, spoke to His disciples the parable: "A sower went out to sow his seed." Later, He said that He was the "Seed," and, still later that if the seed falling to the ground died, it should bring forth life.

The night had now come when Mary became the sower of seed, for was she not bearing the Eternal Word to the grave where in three days He would break the bonds of death and rise forth to everlasting life? She had borne her Son in many sorrowful journeys before, once through Bethlehem to a stranger's cave; now over Golgotha to a stranger's grave — an eloquent reminder, indeed, that human birth and human death were equally foreign to Him. A few hours before, it seemed that neither heaven nor earth would have Him as He hung between the two, abandoned by the one and rejected by the other. But now under the red light of torches, flaming without smoke in the windless air, the grave receives Him. But it will not be for long, for the grave will soon be Nature's womb giving birth to the first-born of the dead. According to ritual the two Sanhedrists, reciting aloud the psalms for the dead, placed the white-wrapped perfumed body in the cave, closed the door with a great stone, and the soft light of the Paschal moon arose — for the sun had set.

There was only one sacrifice left for Mary to make; only one rich consolation which she could put off, to be utterly poor, and that was to leave her Son in the rocks under the guard of Roman soldiers.

She would keep for herself only one thing — a pierced heart as Simeon's last sword found in it its scabbard. By that token Mary would be the consolation of all those who have lost dear ones; of all mothers who mourn over sons; and of all loved ones who grieve over spouses. She understands sorrows, because she lost more than any one else. Some have lost a mother; others a son; others a spouse; but Mary lost everything, for she lost God.

Mary now leans on John, a symbol of the poor compensation we all are to her and steals a glance at the cross — the first one ever to see hope in it. Tens of thousands of hearts, under her sweet inspiration, have looked on it since, and were glad their hearts were broken by it, that through the rent God's love might enter. From the cross Mary turned her eyes to the city of Jerusalem which her Son would have taken to Himself as a hen gathers her chickens under her wing; it now seemed as disconsolate and forlorn as a bird robbed of its nest. Poor Jerusalem! God had loved it long, but now the cup of its iniquity was filled, and doom was on its way before a generation should pass.

Mary retraces her morning pilgrimage making for the second time the way of the Cross, from the fourteenth station to the first. This time it seemed more terrible than the first, because of the very nature of sorrow. All love tends to unity, and in a love such as that of Jesus and Mary, their two hearts were but as one. No power but death could dare render asunder so exquisite a union — and yet death did it. The result was that when she left Him her heart was rent in two; now that she is left alone, the stream of her life can hardly flow; it is not merely that half her life and love is gone. It is something more than that. It is as if her own fountain had run dry like a summer stream. Their lives were one; their deaths are also one. Her sorrow then was deeper than any sorrow on the earth before; it made her weep not just because she lost Him, but because she loved Him. Hers was a love bent wholly on Jesus; a love greater than all mothers' love, even if they might compact their myriad loves into one intensest nameless act; a love that could bear anything, because what was within her was stronger than anything without; in a word, a love so ecstatic and heavenly that if she could have had her will she would have built all her Tabors on Calvary. With such a love in her heart, who then can doubt that as she tramped over the blood-stained streets of Jerusalem she once more, in tones more enraptured than ever, chanted the Magnificat?

Prayer

Mary, Mother of Sorrows, your Seven Sorrows are like a Holy Mass. In your first sorrow, you were appointed Sacristan by Simeon to keep the Host until the Hour of sacrifice; in your second sorrow, you left the Sacristy to serve the altar as your Son's visit sanctified Egypt; in the third sorrow, you recited the Confiteor at the foot of the altar as your Son recited His Confiteor to the Doctors of the Law; your fourth sorrow was the Offertory as you made the oblation of His Body and Blood on the way to Calvary; your fifth sorrow was the Consecration in which you offered your own body and blood in union with your Son's for the Redemption of the world; your sixth sorrow was the Communion when you received the body of your Son from the altar of the Cross; and your seventh sorrow was the Ite Missa est, as you ended your sorrow with an adieu to the tomb.

Mary, your heart is everything to us; it is as a living altar stone on which the sacrifice is offered; it is the sanctuary lamp which jumps with joy before its God; it is the Server, the beatings of whose broken heart are like the responses of the liturgy; it is the Paschal candle which lights the sanctuary of our souls by the sacrifice of self; it is the thurible which gives the sweet odor of incense as it burns in love for us; it is a whole angelic choir singing voiceless songs into ravished ears of the bleeding Host, Our Lord and Savior Jesus Christ.

Mary, sacristan of souls as you were the sacristan of Jesus, a good life is worth nothing if it be not crowned with a happy death. We shall spend our whole life therefore asking this of you, if it be only to gain it at the end. Your Divine Son said He would not leave us orphans. But, Mary, we will be orphans unless you are our Mother.

ETERNAL LIFE

XV

Eternal Life

A s the Church chants her Alleluias and the dead things rise to life, in token of the Resurrection of Our Lord and Savior there is one great thought to be borne in mind, and that is: *what we call life is only death*. The only life is the life of the Risen King.

What do men call life? They call life that temporary endowment of vital forces which animates their body, sees in their eyes, hears in their ears and thrills in their hearts. Death is its opposite or the cessation of all those processes which made living a joy; it is a muffling of the heartbeats, which like a drum on a funeral march becomes silent at the grave. That is what men call death. And it was in the light of such a narrow concept that men judged the majestic Person of Christ. They thought His life ended in death.

In the beginning of His public life, in the first flush of apostolic success the Apostles left their nets, boats and custom tables and flocked to Him as the restorer of the Kingdom of Israel. Judas saw it as a successful financial venture; James and John saw in it an opportunity to sit at His right and at His left in earthly glory; the others jealous of their brethren, quarreled for the first places at table. The power to cast out devils, the thrill of daily companionings with such a noble personage, the peace which stole into their hearts as His words took the wings of angels, and the glory of His triumphant entrance on Palm Sunday into Jerusalem, made His death seem remote enough to be almost impossible. Even though at the very beginning they heard Him speak of His Resurrection, saying that He would in three days rebuild the temple of His Body which men would destroy; even though they had heard Him say that like another Jonah He would be in "the heart of the earth three days and three nights," they still adhered to a narrow, human and worldly outlook on life and death. That is why Peter was scandalized at the very mention of His death. That too is why when Holy Week came, and death began to raise its menacing hand against His holy Life, they dispersed like sheep when the shepherd is struck. Their Master was about to die! It would be the end of their hopes! Judas felt that since death was inevitable, he would profit on it as he had profited on His life. So he sold his Master for thirty silver coins — a sign that Divine things are always bartered away out of all relation to their true worth. Peter, James and John who saw their Master when His face shone like the sun and

His garments were as snow, now slept in a garden when that face was beaded with crimson drops and His garments were dyed red as wine. In the four trials before the Jewish and Roman judges there was not a single Apostle to speak a word in His defense. As trials made history by their injustice against Justice, Peter warmed himself by a fire, and with an atavistic throwback to his fisherman days, cursed and swore that he never knew the man!

At the foot of the Cross only the Apostle John was present. James, his own brother, was not there! Neither was Peter! They were not there, because they thought all was lost. As the last drops of redemption spilled out from the broken chalice of Redemption, they were convinced that it was only a matter of minutes until His life would end. In the unearthly darkness when the sun hid its face at the passing of light, the friends at the foot of the Cross whispered that He was dying! A moment later they sighed that He was dead! All seemed lost! The grave was about to give its sting. Death had won its victory.

As the lengthening shadows of three crosses cast their sinister brooding sadness over the retreating figures, many a man and woman in Jerusalem that day revived sweet memories of Him. It is a regrettable fact that more flowers are scattered at our death than at our living. They loved Him — there was no doubt of that — but it was with that kind of love which shrinks from showing itself at the foot of a cross.

The Apostles kept the memory of a beautiful Kingdom which like Moses, it seemed, they were to see with their mind's eye, but never to enter. Now that death had come and life had gone, back to their nets and their boats they would go. Three years before that great Master had called them away from fishing to be fishers of men. Now that His Flame died away, at the moment they were about to be lighted by it, they would once more become fishers of fish. What more had they to hope for? Had not He Who they hoped would restore the throne of David, died on a peg, with only thorns for a crown, nails for scepter, and His own blood for royal purple? There was just one word to express their attitude, a human word with a human outlook, and with an horizon no broader than that on which the sun sets: — *Christ is dead.*

Now let us contemplate another scene some days afterwards —possibly a week. Many things had transpired in the meantime. The High Priest had returned to his judgment seat, Pilate to his basin of water, and the Fishermen to their nets. It was now evening; the lake was flecked with white as the stars danced upon it, and the moon sent down its rays like silver grappling hooks to move its tides and all the surges of the seas. Seven followers of the Lord who never could forget the Unforgettable gathered about the little harbor of Capernaum. Their boats with their slanting sails, worn seats, and high red rudders were to them like another home. It seemed as if fishing might be good, now that they had turned from men to fish, and from earth to sea for things to catch. Simon, who was named Peter the Rock by the Master, called down the shores to Thomas, Nathaniel, James, John and two others and said, "I'm going fishing." And they answered back, and the hills echoed it again: "We'll go with you, too" (Jn 21:3). They went into the boat, shoved off, labored all the night and caught nothing. At early morn, as the sun began to crimson the Galilean mountain, they began to row to shore. And as they came near, they saw a Man standing on the bank Who seemed to be waiting for them, but they knew not Who it was. His voice rang out like a silver trumpet as He called to them: "Have you caught any fish?" And they answered, "No!"

"Then He said to them, 'Cast the net to the right side of the boat and you'll find some.' So they cast their net and now they were unable to draw it in because of the number of fish" (Jn 21:5-6). And they all began to tremble as the memory of other days awoke within them. "It's the Lord," whispered John to Peter, and instantly the warm-hearted enthusiast, tightening his fisher's tunic round his loins (for he was stripped), leaped into the sea, swam across the hundred yards which separated him from Our Lord, and cast his dripping self at the feet of the Master, as the others following in the boat dropped the strained but unbroken net with its burden of one hundred and fifty-three fish.

A wood fire was burning on the strand, lighted by the Light of the World. Near it was some bread, and on its glowing embers some broiling fish — a meal prepared by the Creator of the Universe in the midst of His creation. Jesus said to them: "Come and eat." And none of them who were at the meal dared ask Him: "Who are You?" — knowing that it was the Lord.

After they'd eaten this simple repast, the Lord of Heaven and earth turned to Simon Peter and said: "Simon, son of John, do you love Me more than they do?" Peter answered Him: "Yes, Lord, you know that I love You." He said to him: "Feed my lambs!" Again He said to him a second time, "Simon, son of John, do you love Me?" He said to Him: "Yes, Lord, You know that I love You." He said to him: "Tend my sheep!" He said to him a third time: "Simon, son of John, do you love Me?" Peter was distressed because He had said to him a third time: "Do you love Me?" And he said to Him: "Lord, You know all things: You know that I love You." He said to him: "Feed my sheep!" (Jn 21:15-17).

The ordeal was over. For Peter's triple denial on the night of the trial, Our Lord drew forth a triple promise of love. But that was not all. He would remind Peter that love is the key to the meaning of death and life by foretelling the kind of death he would undergo: "Amen, amen I say to you, when you were young you fastened your belt and went where you wanted, but when you're old you'll stretch out your hands and another will fasten you and bring you where you do not wish to go" (Jn 21:18).

Briefly, Our Lord was telling Peter: "Love is not a love of earthly life, but a love of death; because I love you they killed me; because of your love of Me, they will kill you. The reward of your labors will be two cross-beams and four nails as I had, but also life eternal." Many years would pass before Peter would be so girded, and before he would recognize himself as so unworthy of his Master, that he would ask to be crucified upside down; but from now on Peter understood something. Mary Magdalene, Mary His Mother, the other Apostles understood it too. It was the tremendous lesson of the Resurrection that every follower of Christ would understand until the end of the world, the lesson that meant unlearning all the wisdom the world ever taught and will ever teach, that lesson which still thrills our hearts today: *It was not Christ who died; it was Death.*

The Resurrection was a fact. He said He would rise again. And He did rise again! *Resurrexit sicut dixit!* Oh! Think not that Peter and the Apostles were the victims of a delusion; think not they had an hallucination and mistook their subjective ideas for the manifestation of the Conqueror of Death. All those who saw the One Whom they thought dead walk in the newness of life had to be convinced. They were not even expecting the Resurrection. The absence of the Apostles at the crucifixion and the other facts mentioned above prove they thought Death ended all. On Easter morning the women went to the sepulcher not to meet the Risen Christ, but to embalm the body. Their greatest worry was who would roll away the stone from the door of the sepulcher; even when they found it rolled away, they did not suppose a Resurrection but only a shameful theft of the body. The message of the angel inspires them not with faith, but with fear and horror.

The Apostles had the same state of mind — the one thing they were afraid of was an hallucination. Hence when the women announced the Resurrection, instead of being impressed they regarded the words of women as "idle tales and believed them not"; Peter and John verified the empty tomb but still knew not the Scriptures concerning the Resurrection. Why, they were so far away from the idea of seeing Him upset the human concept of Death, that when they first saw Him, they thought they had seen a ghost. Mary Magdalene thought He was the gardener, and the disciples on the way to Emmaus did not recognize Him until the breaking of bread. And when they told the other disciples, they were not believed. When He appeared in Galilee, Matthew tells us that some doubted. The very evening of the Resurrection some of His Apostles would not even believe their own eyes until they saw Him eating. Thomas even then doubted and would not be convinced until he put finger unto His Hand, and his hand into the Divine Side to be cured of his doubt and made the Hope and Healer of Agnostics until the end of time.

If His followers were expecting Him, they would have believed at once. If they did finally believe, it was only because the sheer weight of external evidence was too strong to resist. They had to be convinced, and they were convinced. They had to admit their views on death were wrong — Christ was not dead. Life then does not mean what men call life. Hence the world and its ideas had to be remade — for here was a force greater than Nature! Nature had not finished her accounting with Him for Nature received the only serious blow it ever received — the mortal wound of an empty tomb; enemies had not finished their accounting with Him, for they who slew the foe found they had lost their day. Humanity has not finished its accounting, for He came from a grave to show the breast where a Roman spear had forever made visible the Heart which loved men enough to die for them, and then live on in order to love forever; the human mind has not finished its last accounting, for it now has to learn that what men call life is only death, that bodily life is not true life, that he who gives up his soul ruins also the flesh which houses it — in a word, *it was not Christ who died; it was Death.*

Think for a moment on the conduct of the Apostles before the Resurrection, and the way they acted when the Spirit gave them the fullness of belief in the Risen Savior. What new force so transformed the souls of the Apostles, so as to make the abject, the venerated; the ignorant, masters; the egotists, the devoted; and the despairing, saints? What power was it that laid hold of Peter who once said he knew not the man, and now before a learned audience of Parthians and Medes and Elamites, of Mesopotamians, Phrygians and Egyptians and Romans, arises to startle their hearts and thrill their souls with the message, "You killed the Author of Life, Whom God then raised from the dead… So repent and be baptized every one of you in the name of Jesus Christ for the remission of sins" (Ac 3:15, 19). What hand was it that laid hold of Saul, the bitter enemy of Christians, converted him into a Paul and the preacher who counted all things as naught save the glory of the Risen Christ? What new spirit entered into that crude, fish-smelling group of Galilean fishermen which compelled them to go to the capital of the world, which brushed them aside with disdain, and there preach the seemingly grotesque creed that He who was executed as a common criminal by a Roman Procurator was the Resurrection and the Life? Why, that idea was more absurd to the Romans than the idea of a Perfect Supreme God is today to H.G. Wells, or the ideal of purity is to Bertrand Russell! Some new dynamics, some new colossal power had to enter into such simple souls to disrupt a Jewish world and impress itself in twenty years on the entire shore of the Mediterranean from Caesarea to Troas. There is only one force in the world which explains how habitual doubters like Thomas, sensitive tax-gatherers like Matthew, dull men like Philip, impetuous characters like Peter, gentle dreamers like John, and a few seafaring men reeling under the shock of a crucifixion, could be transformed into men of fire, ready to suffer, dare, and if need be to die — and that is the force of love which showed itself in the Christ Whom the builders rejected, and Who now was made the head of the corner. Everywhere, they gave the secret of their success: they were witnesses of a Resurrection; He Who was dead, lives. And eleven of them went out to have their throats cut in testimony of that belief — and men generally do not have their throats cut for an hallucination. There was only one conclusion their blood will let us draw and that is the lesson of Easter Day which they preached — *It was not Christ who died; it was Death.*

The cycles of the years whirl away into history, but it was ever the same antiphon that went up from the hearts of men. Each age repeated it in its own way so that no generation of men was without the tidings of victory. See how that lesson was verified as the followers of the Risen Christ taught Rome the real reason why it was eternal. Hardly grown to their full stature, Nero published his famous edict: "Let there be no Christians!" And his successors, with no fear of God to restrain their cruelty, and a great army to administer it, set to work to destroy the Gospel of the Risen Savior. The swords of the executioners, blunted with slaughter, no longer fitted their sheaths; the wild beasts satiated with Christian blood shrank from it as if more conscious of its dignity than those who ordered it spilt; the river of the Tiber ran red as if already one of the angels of the Apocalypse had poured into it the vial which turns water into blood. A thousand times from a thousand throats there came the cry: "The Christians must die," as a thousand times a thousand thumbs turned down in a signal of death. A day finally came when Rome thought it had cut off the last hand that would make the sign of the Cross and silenced the last tongue that would breathe the name of the risen Christ — and yet what is the verdict of history? The verdict of history is the verdict of the empty tomb. It was the same antiphon struck on a different key. It was not the Christians who died. It was the Roman Empire. *It was not Christ who died; it was Death.*

Come closer to our own times and see Easter once more proclaiming its lesson when men would dare forget even the name. The end of the nineteenth century marked the great upward climb of man divorced from God. Every one of the sacred truths taught by the Church since the first Easter Day was presumed to have been dissolved by the acids of modernity. God was reduced to a mental symbol and then explained away psychologically; man was reduced to an animal and then explained away biologically; life was reduced to chemicals and then explained away mechanically. The supernatural was made synonymous with the superstitious; the mystical identified with the mystified; Christ was a mere social reformer like Buddha and Confucius; the Church was a sect, and man was on the way to being a God.

But just at that moment when the world boasted of its superior organization, its faith in the material and its doubt in the spiritual; just at that very second when it was said the death of the Church marked the beginning of the modern world, the crust of the earth seemed to crack as hell came to the surface in a World War. Science which was supposed to be an ally of man, became his enemy; man who was taught he was only a beast, acted like one; souls that were counted as straw were now blown like chaff across the battlefields of blood; God who was denied now left man to godlessness whose other name is death.

And finally when the smoke of battle cleared away, and the long-range guns were beaten into plowshares and the living made an inventory of the dead, it was discovered that men had failed, that governments had failed, and that institutions had failed. There was only one thing that did not fail; it was the Church and its unwavering loyalty to the Divinity of Christ. The antiphon of Easter was ringing again, only it was struck in a different key. It was not the Church which died; it was the Modern World. *It was not Christ who died; it was Death!*

Now enter into your own personal lives. You have heard the voice of the Eternal Galilean calling to your own heart, as the abyss of goodness cries unto an abyss of need, beckoning you on to His Way, His Truth and His Life. In a moment of silence perhaps — He whispered to you that Truth is in His Church; in an uneasy conscience perhaps He beckoned you to His confessional; in a passing prayer He called you to greater prayerfulness. But you felt it would seem to be the end of your reason if you accepted the Word of Christ in its fullness, that it would be a lowering of your self-respect if you knelt for forgiveness, and that it would be torture to give up the world for deeper and longer prayers. Then finally you took the great step and made the great adventure. You accepted the Truth, you confessed your sins, you perfected your spiritual life, and lo and behold, in those moments when you thought you were losing everything, you found everything; when you thought you were going into your grave,

you were walking in the newness of life; and when
you thought you were in the dark, you were ablaze
with the Light of God. The whole experience of
conversion, confession, sanctification seemed in the
beginning as if you were dead, but it was only a new
verse to an old theme. It was the antiphon of the
empty tomb struck on the chords of your heart by
the fingers of God. It was not you who died; it was
sin. *It was not Christ who died, it was Death.*

Christ lives! The Eternal Galilean abides. Why
then do we not recognize Him? Why do we delay in
embracing the inevitable which is God? There is
nothing new to be tried. There is no need of setting
up new laboratories to test new faiths. We have tried
them all and found them to be old errors with new
labels. We tried all the experiments of the ancients
who believed in the supremacy of man and found
that if we did not believe in God we could not be
human; we tried human fierceness, and it turned
our poppy fields into Haceldamas of blood; we tried
indifference, and it ended in our identification of the
spirit of truth with the specter of evil; we tried
science, and it fed our minds and starved our hearts;
we weighed the earth, measured the turning of
Arcturus and took a census of the stars, set our
thermometers in the very heart of the sun, and in the
end we had new measures, greater numbers and
fancy names, but we still had our ignorance and our
heartaches, and our "dismal universal hiss of sin";

we tried the experiment of law, and we did not obey the law, but changed the law to suit our moods and called it progress; we tried the economic, leaned on its staff and found it pierced our hands; we tried the experiment of Beauty, and found it vanished as we touched it and grew old as we embraced it; we tried the experiment of doubt, and found that if we doubted our doubt we were in "confusion worse confounded"; we tried the experiment of Wealth and found ourselves poorer; the experiment of Power and found ourselves weaker; the experiment of Pride and found ourselves humbled. We found no welcoming shade by quiet waters, where our bodies could repose and our minds could be at rest; we are always seeking but never finding; always knocking and never being admitted; always learning and never coming to a knowledge of truth. There is only one experiment that modern man has not definitely, really tried, and that is the love, not of Jesus the Teacher, Jesus the social reformer, Jesus the humanitarian, but of Him Who is true God and true man, Our Lord and Savior Jesus Christ. Somewhere on earth His unerring absolute Truth still abides; somewhere on earth His Divine Life flows out into hearts like fresh springs from an Eternal Fountain; somewhere on earth His Calvary is prolonged through space and time as other mothers raise up other Johns to stand beneath a cross to swing it in benediction in the direction of Eden's fourfold river;

somewhere Christ lives, loves and teaches. And where that beautiful somewhere is, three hundred million souls on this earth know; but where the other sheep know not through no fault of their own: That beautiful somewhere is the Church or the Mystical Body of Christ.

From the Reviews

"Sheen is blessed with the happy faculty of being able to present the sublime mysteries of the Christian Gospel in a language the modern age understands." *Catholic World*

"A beautifully written life of Christ and one that might almost be called a modern version, comes from the prolific pen of Fulton J. Sheen. It is entirely different in its treatment and yet the author knows well how to present his subject in a language easily understandable to the world of today... Here is a volume that may well serve as an inspiration to the many readers who find this author's works penetrating and enlightening." *Boston Post*

"Full of insight and valuable suggestions for all." *Ave Maria*

"The pages breathe a deep love of Christ whom the writer portrays appealingly as alone having a solution for man's many troubles and difficulties. Retelling the life of One who was a Galilean and lived in that small country 2,000 years ago, Bishop Sheen shows that Christ still lives, still vivifies and energizes those who seek and find Him, still dominates every heart into which He is allowed entrance." *America*

"In this book Bishop Sheen tells the story of the Son of God. But he does more than relate history; he portrays some of the characteristics of the Eternal Galilean—that Divine Person made Man in Nazareth... The doings and the teachings of Our Lord are told in language nicely adapted to the nuances of the author's thought. An occasional play on words, a well-turned sentence, an excellent choice of words throughout, combine to make his learned work a pleasant, and almost poetic, piece of soteriological literature." *Catholic Historical Review*

"A devout and beautifully written life of Christ, a book to be appreciated and enjoyed by all Christians, whether Catholic or not." *Hartford Courant*

"A perfect sample of readable religion." *Catholic Tribune*